Modern Methods of Middle School Teaching: *Reaching Special Education Students*

by

Karl M. Knutson

PublishAmerica
Baltimore

Ron & Kathy — You are now in an elite group - you are among the few to have bought this book! Best regards, Karl Knutson 6-22-08

First printing

ISBN: 1-4137-1364-5
PUBLISHED BY PUBLISHAMERICA, LLLP
www.publishamerica.com
Baltimore

Printed in the United States of America

To Suzy

TABLE OF CONTENTS

Introduction	p. 6
Chapter 1 : *What is Special Education All About?*	p. 11
Chapter 2: *Classroom Management*	p. 25
Chapter 3: *Is Reading a Religion?*	p. 33
Chapter 4: *The Journey to Better Writing Is an Ego Trip*	p. 41
Chapter 5: *Creative Ways to Teach Math*	p. 53
Chapter 6: *Making Social Studies Fun*	p. 85
Chapter 7: *Science is...Experiments!*	p. 99
Chapter 8: *What's it all about, LD?*	p. 105

INTRODUCTION

That special education teachers experience a "burn-out" is an observable phenomenon. In order to keep the attention of growing numbers of special education students, the teacher expends a great deal of energy. This takes its toll on both the body and the psyche of teachers whose purpose for going into special education was to lead young people with special needs towards attaining educational and personal fulfillment. When the students do not embrace the lofty goals and creative preparation employed by the teacher, it can be disheartening and demoralizing. The same is true of general education.

This book can change your life. It was written to share some ideas that were developed literally for survival during a year in which 20 special education sixth-graders were assigned to this teacher in a room that was 18-by-25 feet. It was a multicategorical model in which there were students with various needs associated with learning, mental, and behavioral disabilities. All subjects were taught in an academic block from 8:00 a.m. to 11:30 a.m. Language arts, math, science, and social studies were the subjects. Classroom control and learning were the overall objectives.

Several myths are debunked in this book. Many teachers think that they will lose students who have difficulty reading if they use grade-level textbooks in their instruction. On the contrary, with methodologies portrayed in this book, the special education or general education teacher will find a new world of supportive resources that heretofore were not employed because of negative- or false-thinking about textbooks. Textbooks contain great amounts of information and should be utilized.

Consider this a "how-to" book written by a teacher in the trenches, not a publish-or-perish purveyor of pedantry up in an ivory tower. After struggling through innumerable articles and books in the pursuit of a degree, you will find this a useful, refreshing read. Unlike some college textbooks and professional articles, it does not have writing in which the goal seems to be to convolute a sentence and impress the colleagues. There are many life-saving (both your life and your students') techniques contained in this book. It is based on experience and the truism that everyone likes recognition and learning new things. Teaching is a noble profession. Doctors work with sick people, lawyers often work with criminals, but teachers have the gallant opportunity of helping young people on a difficult journey. Teachers do not make a sale for profit. They profit by helping others.

Ode to Teachers

Oh hallowed halls of learning ring
A plangent echo of promise bring.
And tho' your stay ephemeral be,
You toll the bell of truths to see.

Karl Knutson

Chapter One
What Is Special Education All About?

HISTORY

In 1957, a bombshell hit the United States. No, it wasn't an actual bomb, but its impact resounded over the length and breadth of this country. The Russians, then known as the Soviet Union, had launched a successful orbiting satellite called "Sputnik." Prior to this, American scientists had touted 1957 as their "International Geophysical Year". This initiative to understand more about the world by using weather balloons and oceanographic equipment was completely overshadowed by the little beeping satellite that the Russians had orbiting the Earth, right over our territory!

What was our country doing wrong? How was the Soviet Union able to pass us by? As the pundits looked for answers they began to question the American education system. Were we not expecting enough of our schools? Critics said the people of America were too complacent. Standards should be elevated.

Expectations were raised, especially in mathematics and science, and new reading norms were established. There was also a "social expectation that schools help America's cold war effort and also sort students for future work roles in a stratified economy" (Sleeter, 1986, p. 48). Many students were unable to keep up with higher reading demands, but nobody attributed that to the new reading norms. By the early 1960's, those who couldn't keep up in reading skills were grouped in five categories by educators. Some were MR (mentally retarded – now called MD for persons with a mental disability) on the basis of IQ scores. A group that had a slightly higher IQ than the MRs were called "slow learners." Two other groups were categorized as "socially maladjusted" and "emotionally disturbed." For reasons unknown, these two groups were mostly populated by students of low-income backgrounds, such as African and Puerto Rican descent. A fifth group came to be known as the learning disabled (Sleeter, 1986). These groups were more clearly defined and expanded upon in Federal legislation of 1975.

The LD (Learning Disabled) category was glaringly devoid of black students during the category's first ten years, and the MR groups had a higher percentage of black students than the general population (Sleeter, 1986). Early structuring of the LD group enabled white, middle-class parents to explain that their failing child was in fact "different" from the lower-class students typically categorized as MR, thus ensuring more help and attention for their own child and preserving the "superiority" of the white middle-class culture. It is indicative of entrenched racism that black learning problems were called "mental retardation," and white learning problems were due to "a slight brain dysfunction" that required some special training. Can't you just hear some of the parents in their white neighborhood schools saying that "Johnny just has a learning problem and needs some special attention; he really does have a high IQ, you know."

Contrary to the language school officials used about always having their students' best interests in mind, the reformation of these disparities did not take place from within the hallowed halls of learning. Educators did not give any attention to children of diverse backgrounds except to categorize them in order to explain failure until Federal legislation was enacted to push equality in public school systems. All of the changes made to meet the needs of educating society have been the result of court cases and Federal legislation. In *Brown v. Topeka, Kansas Board of Education (1954)*, segregation for students by race was found to be unconstitutional. In *Pennsylvania Association for Retarded Citizens (PARC) v. Commonwealth of Pennsylvania (1971)*, it was judged that schools in Pennsylvania must provide free, public education to all school-age retarded children. The case of *Mills v. Board of Education of the District of Columbia (1972)* found that keeping individuals with disabilities from free, appropriate public education was contrary to due process and equal protection clauses of the Fourteenth Amendment to the Constitution (Hardman, 1993). The Fourteenth Amendment, Section 1 outlines rights of all people born or naturalized in the United States, and continues, "No state shall make or enforce any law which shall abridge the privileges or immunities of citizens of the United States; nor shall any state deprive any person of life, liberty, or property, without due process of law; nor deny to any person within its jurisdiction the equal protection of the laws" (*The Constitution of the United States of America).*

Naturally, in a democracy such as the United States, the laws and the institutions should reflect the will and the needs of the people. Also, a democracy will not work without a populace that is knowledgeable enough to make rational decisions, such as electing representatives and acting on referenda. The legal system depends on a jury that is able to arrive at conclusions based on the facts. By constitutional default, it is up to the states to provide for the education of its citizens. Historically, however, this education has been found wanting. Some segments of our society, especially the African-Americans of the southern regions, see "states' rights" as a white code word for keeping minorities as second-class citizens.

Changes in education continued to come about through Federal legislation. In the 1970's, the rights of individuals with disabilities was addressed. Public Law 93-112, Vocational Rehabilitation Act of 1973, Section 504 declared that persons with disabilities cannot be excluded form participation in, denied benefits of, or subjected to discrimination under any program or activity receiving Federal financial assistance (Hardman, 1993). This gave the Federal government clout over the local school districts since the carrot on a stick being offered was the Federal monetary assistance so many school systems had come to depend on. Section 504, to this day, has been the source of confusion regarding the nebulous line between itself and subsequent special education legislation.

Public Law 93-380, Educational Amendments Act of 1974 provided financial aid to the states for implementation of programs for children who are exceptional, including the gifted and talented. Due-process requirements were established to protect the rights of children with disabilities and their families in special education placement decisions. (Hardman, 1993).

In 1975, Congress saw fit to bring together all the different Federal and states' laws into an all-encompassing, national law. Hence, Public Law 94-142, or Part B of the Education of the Handicapped Act (EHA) made available a *free and appropriate public education* (FAPE) to students with disabilities in the United States. It mandated that all eligible students, regardless of the extent or type of handicap, were to receive, at public expense, the special education services necessary to meet their individual needs. These services included specially designed instruction in the classroom, home, or hospital. This legislation formulated the basis for special education today. It established the IEP (individualized education program), named eligibility requirements for special education services, such as persons who were mentally retarded, hard-of-hearing, visually impaired, speech impaired, seriously emotionally disturbed, orthopedically impaired, other health impaired, or learning disabled. There was no language regarding attention deficit disorders. It defined related services, such as transportation, speech pathology, psychological services, physical and occupation therapy, recreation and medical services needed for a disabled child to benefit from special education (Hardman, 1993).

There followed three acts from 1986 to 1990 that spelled out early interventions with infants and toddlers, reimbursement of attorneys' fees to parents who prevail in administrative and court actions, and civil rights protections in private-sector employment, public accommodations, transportation, and telecommunications. (Hardman, 1993).

The 1975 legislation, PL 94-142 (EHA) was amended in 1990 by Public Law 101-476, and was called the Individuals with Disabilities Education Act, or IDEA. This expanded the special education program outlined in PL 94-142 in a number of ways. Traumatic brain injuries and autism were added to the list of eligible conditions for special education services. The IEP now had to include transition services statements for students by age 16. The definition of special education was expanded from classroom, home, or hospital to include instruction in all settings such as the workplace and training centers. Finally, it required the U.S. Department of Education to study the issue of providing special education to students with attention deficit disorder, or ADD (Hardman, 1993).

In May of 1997, Congress re-authorized IDEA, now known as IDEA 97. It addressed a number of issues. The high points of IDEA are: (1) Students with disabilities should be tied as much as possible to the general education curriculum and assessments. Also, the LRE (Least Restrictive Environment) should be emphasized in such a way that interventions are done which allow the students to be successful in the general education environment as much as possible. (2) Student progress in special education should be assessed and reported as often as the general education students. (3) District-wide assessments should include special education students' participation, or identify appropriate accommodations. (4) The IEP Team must include at least one general education teacher, who will attend the IEP meetings. The IEPs should have statements of measurable annual goals and explain general education participation. (5) Suspending students beyond 10 days may occur only if it does not establish a pattern. The last item above attempts to deal with the threat of dangerous weapons and drugs. One of the possibilities for dealing with unruly or dangerous students is a 45-day placement in what many school districts call an Alternative Education Center. These Centers meet the requirements of schooling as it serves as an attendance center for those students experiencing behavioral difficulties and are under suspension (Mueller, 1999).

The Vocational Rehabilitation Act, Section 504, alluded to above, had nothing to do with special education. It was developed for students and is enforced by the Office of Civil Rights. IDEA is enforced by the United States Office of Special Education Programs. Students that are qualified in IDEA are categorized under one or more of the thirteen disabling conditions. Specially designed individual education programs are planned for each student by IEP teams. Section 504 is a broad civil rights law that protects the rights of individuals with handicaps. Any student with a substantial mental or physical impairment that limits one or more of the his/her major life activities is eligible for a 504 accommodation plan. Examples of potential 504 handicapping conditions not typically covered under IDEA are communicable diseases, such as HIV, tuberculosis, asthma, and diabetes. Attention Deficit Disorder (ADD) and Attention Deficit Hyperactivity Disorder (ADHD) are eligible in 504, but are not listed in one of the 13 eligible disabilities for special education. Section 504 does not require a written IEP document but does require a plan. The plan may address an "appropriate" education program that is comparable to the education provided to non-handicapped students, such as building and program accessibility. Related services, independent of any special education services as defined under IDEA, may be the reasonable accommodation. Section 504 does not provide additional funds to school districts. IDEA funds may not be used to serve children found eligible only under Section 504. Finally, in this brief comparison of IDEA and Section 504, participation in IDEA's special education requires parental or guardian consent, whereas Section 504 does not.

The lines between special education's IDEA legislation and Section 504 of the Vocation Rehabilitation Act may be a little unclear to the uninitiated. However, it hardly compares to the level of debate between educators when discussing the suitability of a child's placement into special education.

PLACEMENT

Placement into special education was supposed to be determined by employing various interventions by a multi-disciplinary team, which would then arrive at a collective decision. The categories for administering special education are: learning disability (LD), mental disability (MD), behavioral disability (BD), and physical disabilities. Learning disability is the most difficult to assess and agree upon. "Discrepancy" used to be the main criterion for identifying a learning disability. Discrepancy was the phenomenon of low performance in one of the academic disciplines. Discrepancy occurs when the student's performance is not in keeping with expected performance as indicated by various predicting devices, such as an IQ test. If the child was determined to be average or above average in intelligence, but his/her performance in the language skills of reading, writing, listening, and speaking are low, then discrepancy was evident thereby meeting one of the assessment criterions for a learning disability. Other academic areas of achievement that are weighed are math calculation, reasoning skills, and cognitive ability. Supposedly, the multi-disciplinary team could not assess discrepancy on the basis of visual, hearing or motor disability as well as emotional disturbance, mental retardation, and environmental, cultural, or economic disadvantage.

In many middle schools today, students who need help to survive in school are grouped together in a multi-categorical model. This is an economically necessary method for teaching students of several different disabilities in one classroom. In this model, a class in special education language arts could inlcude students with learning, mental, or behavioral disabilities. The students with a mental disability and a behavioral disability are placed in a less restrictive educational environment with students of a learning disability. This is due to a determination that,while they need special instruction, their degree of disability is not such that they require a more restrictive class including all mental disabilities or all behavioral disabilities. The various levels of restrictions are given numerical values by which Federal funding is granted. The least restrictive class, such as the multi-categorical class, is given weight of 1.7. Slightly increased restriction in a homogenous grouping of either MD or BD is weighted at 2.7. More restriction is assigned a weight of 3.6. Recently, these three strata were categorized as Level 1, Level 2, and Level 3, presumably to pigeonhole wide varieties of behaviors—academic and social—into groups for managing.

It's a numbers game. Not only are the various levels weighted, but the number of students at each level may influence, for better or worse, the number of students in each program. For example, the 3.6 BD program should have five to eight students per teacher. So, a student with behavioral problems may be kept at a Level 2 because there is no room in the more restrictive Level 3 BD program. Likewise, the same relationship may be present between Levels 1 and 2, even between general education and special education for that matter. In reality, however, all the levels are becoming more crowded as low-performering students become more numerous and special education is perceived to be the answer. In fact, an all-encompassing "entitled individual" is the new phrase used in the IEP to expedite a child with a disability's placement in special education .

According to the Lexington Institute in Arlington, Virginia, about 12% of children in U.S. schools are enrolled in special education (Soifer, 2002). This is misleading information regarding the number of students requiring special education in the U.S., because private schools are not required to have special education programs. In the public middle schools, it is more like 25% of the students are enrolled in special education. In the fall of 2002, this author had 24 out of 96 sixth-graders on a special education roster. In the fall of 2003, there are 22 out of 102 students on the the author's roster of Level 1 special education, LD-type students. The list will be added to as the year progresses. The number does not reflect the Level 2 students with a mental disability in this author's middle school building.

Generally, the elementary schools pull out students with disabilities at scheduled times during the day to have special sessions on various academic subjects with a special education teacher. In the middle schools, as cited above, special education teachers have classes of students with disabilities, primarily with reading and written expression deficits. Some classes are for those students with a math disability. For other subjects, the special education teachers may go with some of their students as they attend general education classes, such as science and social studies, where they work in conjunction with the general education teacher to give assistance to their charges. Furthermore, there are some students in the more restricted environments that attend selected general education classes or less restricted classes based on their ability to survive or as a result of good performance. In the high schools, the special education department is usually the largest of all the academic departments. A variety of plans are employed for the needs of special education students to meet the goals of graduation and transition for life after high school.

Placement of a student into special education from pre-referral to an IEP was designed to work as follows (paraphrased from Mercer, C.D. (1987). *Students with learning disabilities* 3rd ed.), Columbus, OH: Merrill):

> *Pre-referral:* In order to reduce the number of referrals into special education, pre-referral is gaining in functional use to screen potentially labeled students using other avenues of intervention. Brainstorming by general education teachers or a combination of general education teachers and special education teachers can result in strategies for instruction or remediation. The pre-referrals provide the opportunity for increased communication within a school that may lead to effective treatments in the general education classroom.
>
> *Referral:* If this step is warranted, information is gathered about a child in order to arrive at intelligent decisions regarding his/her future. The group to which a child has been referred is a multi-disciplinary team of various components. It could be a dozen professionals, including a social worker, a reading specialist, special educators, general educators, area support personnel, a psychologist, school administrators, and a nurse. Before making an assessment, the team may recommend more behavior observations or documentation regarding why the student has been referred to them.
>
> *Assessment for identification:* The information gathered by the team, including behavior observations, psychological and intelligence testing, physical abilities, home visits by the social worker, and academic achievement discussions, is put to use

after parental permission has been granted. For academic level assessment, there are several commercial batteries of math and reading achievement tests available, as well as innate intelligence measurements employed by the psychologist such as the *WISC-R* and *Stanford-Binet Intelligence Scale.* If discrepancy is found to be a factor (i.e., there is poor achievement in relation to the assessed ability level of the student) the student could be identified as having a learning disability, provided the low performance is not attributable to mental retardation, physical impairment, emotional disturbance, or environmental/cultural factors. If IQ is determined to be a qualifying factor, a mental disability could be identified. Behavioral problems could result in the student being identified with a behavioral disability, in which case the psychologist would have employed a personality scale in the assessment as well as a good deal of observation data. The team should weigh the data as to the reliability and validity of the measurements. Other factors should also be considered, such as length of duration of suspected disability and the determination of whether problems are only setting-specific.

Initial Assessment for Instruction: The key components of this level are what to teach and how. Or, in the usual working lexicon of special education, determine what the goal areas should be as outlined in an IEP. Determine the scope and sequence of skills to be taught. Decide what behavior to assess. Select an evaluation activity. For example, some teacher-made devices could be utilized to evaluate cognitive ability in math. Translated into a long-term objective, the special education teacher might write on an IEP, "The student will perform two-digit integer calculations of addition and subtraction with 90% accuracy." The *how* of what to teach is what facilitates instruction. Knowing how to teach an objective encompasses expectancy factors, stimulus events, response factors, and subsequent events. Lesson plans may be written after this has been considered.

IEP (Individualized Education Program): In addition to multidisciplinary assessment and parental approval, the IEP is mandated. This provides a vehicle for parents and professionals to work together in determining an appropriate educational plan for the student's education. When there is agreement regarding a student's disability, a directional process for instruction is established which is the essence of the IEP. The IEP meeting is attended at minimum by the special education teacher, a general education teacher, an administrator or designee, the child, parent(s), and a school counselor. During the meeting, the present level of educational performance (PLEP) is discussed. The annual goals are determined. This may be a collective process, but realistically the special education teachers have goals in mind and will generally have such goals in writing as a proposal. These goals are generally approved. Any change of placement must have parental approval. The IEP is reviewed annually by the appropriate teachers for continuation of the instructional plan and overall compliance is determined for the benefit of the student. Of course, a new IEP can be called for at any time before a year is up, depending on the needs of the student.

PLACEMENT MOTIVATIONS

If every student with below-level reading scores or math scores were to be placed in special education,there would be more special education students than general education students in many school districts. American schools cannot simply send kids into special education because of poor reading performance. Some educators entertain misconceptions of special education as a place to send children who are not making the grade in the general curriculum. State education departments, through area education agencies, have made initiatives towards educating the public school districts about employing interventions that help students thrive or at least improve performances in traditional school environments. To this end, all schools have multi-disciplinary teams, under many different names, to try different ways of keeping students on the path of success. A school might call their child study team STEP (Student/Team Educational Planners), or ISAP (Individual Student Action Plan). They meet weekly to discuss an agenda of students who are failing or are a disruptive element in a classroom. They begin to document a baseline of data and interventions employed in bringing a student into a level of adequate achievement.

Many teachers view the weekly team meetings as a venue for documenting difficult students into special education. These are the teachers who present the lessons and assign homework, placing blame and responsibility on the student should their work fall below expectation. Personal commitment, by which a teacher helps the students along with motivations and a human touch, does wonders. It could be as simple as a verbal reinforcement ("Way to go!") when a student gets their homework done. Unfortunately, there is a mind-set that expresses the belief that since the advent of special education, especially the category of learning disability, teachers are no longer required to go to extraordinary lengths to keep a student on track. They lobby for difficult students to be placed into special education, an action that is usually masked as a noble concern for getting the student some help.

Because of teacher unions, principals are reluctant to show a lack of support for a teacher. They follow the path of least resistance. If passing a student on to special education means less disciplinary interventions for fractious students or keeping failing grades at a minimum, the administrators view such alternatives as having a positive effect. Instead of counseling faculty on teaching methods or offering suggestions regarding motivational techniques, the administrators are party to creating special education classes that are much too large. Rod Paige, the Secretary of Education, has made it known that he feels schools systems do not provide basic skills education such as reading, resulting in about half of the special education students being placed there in error (Soifer, 1999).

The way special education was created to work was in order for students who do not thrive in the general academic setting after various interventions have been tried are to be tested by the school psychologist in order to determine if the student has a disability. What is problematic is that there is not enough time in a school year for the psychologist, who is responsible for a half dozen schools, to test every candidate for special education. So, a curriculum-based assessment was developed to provide the means by which a child's candidacy for special education is determined. In other words, if a child is getting bad grades, doesn't read well, shows a lack of proficiency in math, or doesn't do his/her homework, then he/she must be a special education student. In this sense, the learning disability aspect of special education legislation of the 1970's failed. Creators of the law did not foresee that such a nebulous, undefined category would be embraced by general educators as a way of avoiding the development of innovative, creative, and flexible teaching methods to meet the wide variety of needs that a classroom of students represents today.

What can be done about this? First of all the administrators, i.e. the principals, associate principals, and facilitators, must take a more active role in teaching. Most of their day is taken up with dealing with discipline problems in order to support the teachers. They should be involved with what information is being taught and how it is being taught. They must know what is going on in the classrooms. If a teacher frequently employs non-teaching activities such as worksheet after worksheet with no student feed-back, copying questions from an overhead projector, or similar busy work while remaining at their computer, it is not unexpected for a student to misbehave. The administrators should be aware of the teacher's procedures when a student has been sent to the office because he/she won't do the work or is being unmanageable. Conversely, there are many very good teachers who establish a connection with their students. They engage their charges in a variety of activities. They encourage them and follow their progress. Teachers like this would make a principal's job much easier. I once asked a principal how he ran such a good school. He said, "I hire good teachers."

Another way to get special education on its correct path is for the special education teachers to act as a consultant to general education teachers. Unfortunately, most general education teachers are rarely open to having a colleague suggest that their expectations may be too high for everyone in the class to meet without some teacher flexibility and involvement. The special education teacher has a lot to offer about trying a variety of methods for reaching students. They should share their expertise with the general education teachers, but it cannot be accomplished without the support and leadership of the principal.

This book is about sharing tried and true techniques for imparting knowledge, improving academic skills, and maintaining classroom control (even under extremely crowded conditions) without detentions or sending students "to the office." It is based on trial-and-error knowledge gained after 16 years' experience in teaching at the middle school level.

Chapter Two:
Classroom Management

Classroom control should be based on the premise that it is a privilege to be in your class. How do you make it seem like a privilege? Make it interesting and fun so that the students want to be there. How do you make it interesting and fun? Two words: Energy and preparation. In short, you should know where you are going and overwhelm your students with enthusiasm. Don't give them time to be bored or disruptive. Does it sound hard? Believe this: it's a lot less taxing to infuse energy and vivacity into the teaching process than dealing with disruptive students who don't want to be there or do not want to learn anything.

The following techniques of discipline and control work hand-in-glove with all the academic classes. The methods described in the following chapters will not work without first establishing the rules of the game. And, like all games, it is meant to be fun. Therein lies the secret: learning can be fun. You'll find you don't have to chase kids down to make them stay after school as a means for discipline. This book is pursuant to the decision to have classroom control without detentions or "sending kids to the office." First, make a list of all your students in all your classes. Tape it to the chalkboard or put it on a clipboard with easy access, as you will be awarding points often. For example, when you walk into your class and see some students at their desks ready and attentive. Give those students a point along with a compliment like, "Way to be in your seats and ready to go." Keep that in mind: everyone likes to be recognized for doing good things. Be liberal with your compliments. If a student wants to borrow some masking tape for one thing or another, say, "Since you're such a good student—sure." That is your operative word: "Sure." May I go to the bathroom? "Sure." So, not only do you make your class fun, you create an atmosphere of mutual respect. In other words, your classroom becomes a pleasant place.

Table 1

	POINTS LIST
Jarane Abdulahi	𝍸 𝍸 ///
Courtney Anderson	~~𝍸 𝍸~~ 𝍸 𝍸 ///
Cara Atworth	///
Courtnie Benson	𝍸 /
Heather Blanes	50 ~~𝍸 𝍸~~ 𝍸 ///
Mitchell Brown	///
Sheena Carson	////
Heather Crydon	~~20 𝍸~~ 𝍸 𝍸 ///
T.J. Druzchinski	//
Chelsie Dwyer	𝍸 𝍸 𝍸 𝍸 /
Jake Faranbault	𝍸 𝍸 ///
Samantha Fleck	30 ///
Isaac Francis	𝍸 𝍸 𝍸 𝍸 𝍸 //
Teela Fuguera	////
Eva Grandon	~~𝍸 𝍸 𝍸 𝍸~~ 𝍸 𝍸 𝍸 ///
Eric Johansen	///
Ericka Justice	////
Lindsey Kingsworth	~~𝍸 𝍸~~ ////
Anthony Kopel	///
Michael Kristane	𝍸 𝍸 //
Brandon Lopez	~~30~~ ///
Sarah Mahane	𝍸
Erica Meershaum	~~𝍸 𝍸 𝍸~~ 𝍸 𝍸 ///
Nickie Nakasone	𝍸 𝍸 /
D.J. Optiman	𝍸 //
Greg Sanchez	//
Eric Schott	𝍸 𝍸 ///
Paige Turner	///
Alex Vogel	~~𝍸 𝍸~~ 𝍸 𝍸 //
Angel Wadena	///
Chelsea Wharton	~~𝍸 𝍸 𝍸 𝍸 𝍸 𝍸~~ 𝍸 //
Sarena Willi	𝍸
Alvinn Wilson	𝍸 𝍸 ////
Angela Zimmer	𝍸 //

See the "Points Sheet." Notice that some points have been marked off. These points have been "spent," i.e. a student has turned them in for an item of choice. What can they earn? It is really up to the discretion of the teacher as to the value of the various rewards. This teacher has listed some things as follows: Invite a friend up for school lunch, 15 points. A T-shirt provided by a business partner, 20. Computer time for games, 10 to 20 points. A can of soda, 30 points.

A student store coupon, 20 points. Pizza lunch with a friend, 200 points. Free time to walk the halls for 10 minutes, 10 points. Special education budgets at schools usually provide for the purchase of such incentive items.

There are numerous ways points are awarded. It's up to the imagination of the teacher. If it's reading class, give a point for reading aloud. If a student says something to provoke a classmate and the classmate ignores it, give a point and say, "That was very mature of you to not respond to that unkind statement. Way to go." Perhaps you have a couple of minutes of class left and you have accomplished what you wanted. So have the class name a category. A dozen hands go up. You call on somebody and one student says, "Soccer." Pose a question such as, "How many players are on a side in soccer ?" She answers, "Eleven," for which you award a point. Points are an all-day, on-going recognition of positive behavior. By the same token, since a student did something that was good, you cannot undo it by taking away points. Once points have been given, do not take them away for some infraction or for bad behavior.

As students become accustomed to the point system, the teacher can make it easier to award points so that he/she is not constantly going back and forth to the master points list. At the beginning of class, a point-taker can be designated. A good practice is to pick a student that is usually in their seat and raising their hand. The point-taker is given a class list from a stack of preprinted sheets that are a half-page size. Whenever the teacher indicates, the point-taker gives a point to the student on the tally. The teacher might say in a class discussion, "Great answer. Give Ben a point." At the end of class, the point-taker transfers the awarded points from the tally onto the master sheet.

The points are not given for regular academic work, which is graded. But it is helpful to have a lot of extra credit work available for the students to do for points when they are not doing some of the regular classroom work. Keep hundreds of sheets of various topics in an expandable file. These can be math sheets, poetry to memorize, map identification, research questions, word finds, or puzzles to do whenever assigned tasks are completed so your students are kept busy and not getting into trouble. Have a designated box for turning in the extra credit. Periodically, the teacher corrects these accumulated extra credit worksheets and awards the points. Points are commensurate with work done, such that a word find is one or two points, while a research worksheet or a memorized poem would be 20 points or more. Other examples: identifying all the U.S. states on a blank map, 20 points. Naming all the capitals on a blank map, 30 points. Memorizing all the U.S. presidents in order, 30 points.

If at all possible, a request for redeeming points should be honored immediately. If a student wants to buy a piece of candy for 10 points in the middle of class, the teacher should say, "Sure," and allow him or her to get a piece of candy from the candy box. At that time, the number of points redeemed is crossed off the master points list. This maintains the integrity of the system and serves as an incentive for the rest of the class as they observe this positive and rewarding transaction. Of course, some things opted for cannot be done immediately, such as inviting a friend to the classroom for lunch. In essence, the ways to earn points and prizes for same are unlimited and up to the creativity of the teacher. If a student admires a poster in the room, the teacher could say they could own it for a reasonable amount of points.

The point system is an integral part of the discipline that is maintained. It is a privilege to redeem points for an award. If a student has ignored the rules of no talking unless recognized, employed inappropriate language, or commited other infractions, there should be a consequence, or, as the behaviorists would say, a punishment. This is the opposite of the reinforcement described in the point system. Here is a scenario: After a few warnings, Johnny has continued to talk to his neighbor instead of paying attention in class. A sheet on which there are 25 lines underneath a heading that states, "I will follow the rules about talking," is presented to the student. Before Johnny may redeem any points, or enjoy any other privileges, that sheet must be filled out. It doesn't matter when the sheet is filled out, as the teacher may so state, but it must be done. Johnny can still earn points, and in fact, Johnny may be accruing a lot of points before he decides to do the sheet in a couple of days. As points are earned, there is an increased incentive to do the punishment because he may want to spend them, which he cannot do until he has filled out the sheet. Also, a lesson has been learned: do not get another sheet because they are not any fun. This book will not go so far as to say that the repeated sentence, such as, "I will try harder to be punctual," or "I will avoid using inappropriate language," enters the subconscious and subliminally alters behavior, but it is possible.

Usually, it is recommended that the sheet for an offense not be given to the errant student right away at the time of the infraction, because the student may take that as an opportunity to be obstreperous and crumple it up in a moment of defiance. It may suffice to tell the student in question that he has a sheet to fill out anytime he wants to pay the consequences for his/her violation of a rule. A note at the bottom of the points list serves as a reminder that a student must fill out the sheet before points can be redeemed or other privileges enjoyed. It may look like this: "Johnny – Talking." After he has filled out the form, simply cross out the reminder and privileges are restored.

Some bad behavior can be ignored. If a student talks out and asks a question, do not respond. Respond to someone who has raised his/her hand. Make it clear that in order for everyone to be heard, anyone who wants to talk should raise his/her hand and be recognized. You may ignore a student who is not raising his/her hand, and then, when the student does raise his/her hand, reward it immediately by saying something like, "Thanks for raising your hand. You get a point for that." This can work wonders. Other intermittent reinforcement is a powerful tool. For example, sometime when everyone is working hard, the teacher might say, "Wow. Everyone is working so well I'm going to give everybody 2 points right now." Psychologists and behaviorists will attest to the power of intermittent reinforcement.

The students will be on your side when you are fair and show that you honestly like them. Never punish the whole class when a few individuals are misbehaving. To say something like, "I was going to have everybody play a game, but some of you have been talking, so we won't," gives a few individuals power over the rest of the class.

Instead, reward those who are attentive and doing their work to the exclusion of the others who are not. As to honestly liking your students, they will get the idea that you do when you take opportunities to find out about their lives by asking them to share what they did last night or over the week-end and truly listen to them. Start off every day that way and you will be pleasantly surprised.

The classroom control methods described thus far should be adhered to with energy and creativity. Sometimes, for variety, it is effective to have a long-term goal to which the class may aspire. Kids really love pizza and eating together as a group. Once a month, invite the class to bring in a couple of dollars for a pizza lunch that you order to be delivered in your classroom. The kids *love* this and will adhere to a target behavior in order to be invited to the pizza lunch. The target behavior is quietness during a daily resource room study hall so that you can help individuals with their work. A study hall monitor should be assigned on a rotating basis (perhaps a chart on a wall to keep track). During the period, the monitor records a mark by the names of anyone that has talked or made some attention-getting noise on a small chart at the monitor's desk. At the end of the period, the monitor gives the chart to the teacher for recording on the master list. The master list is done by code and everyone is given his/her own secret code. This lends an air of mystery and ownership to the entire venture. Periodically, the coded list is projected on the overhead so that everyone may see how many marks they have accrued. Explain that nobody is perfect and sometimes we forget, but long-term patterns are established so that those that have an egregious tendency of not being quiet will not be invited for the pizza. Marks are a punishment, but the net effect is to reward those that have adhered to the target behavior. It is extremely effective. It allows for mistakes and no one is ruled out except those that need to focus on what is expected the next time. It is so effective that oftentimes everyone is invited for lunch. Experience has indicated that for the pizza lunch reward to be effectrive, it should not be done more than once a month. A good benchmark is that anyone under 20 marks is invited. If they don't make the cut the first time, you can bet they will be most attentive to the rules the next time. It is suggested that when collecting the money, a note be sent home to the parent(s) saying, "As a reward for courteous and attentive behavior in study hall, your child has been invited for a pizza lunch in the classroom. To help defray the cost, a voluntary donation of $2.00 per student is requested." Try it. It is easy to implement and very effective.

To summarize: be fair, have fun, and make your students want to be in your classroom. Overwhelm them with your energy and enthusiasm. Magnify the good behaviors by rewards and positive attention. Be interested in your students and build a positive relationship by treating them with respect and expecting the same in return. Minimize bad behavior by not giving it a disproportionate amount of attention. It is better to "catch a kid being good." Be matter-of-fact in meting out punishments. Do not make disciplinary actions personal attacks, nor should you take unwanted behaviors personally. A reward system and classroom control is instrumental in the methods described in the academic subjects that follow.

Chapter 3
Is Reading a Religion?

At the University of Iowa in Iowa City, Iowa there is a renowned summer reading program that is conducted at the Speech and Hearing Building on campus. Professors from the College of Education instruct prospective degree candidates on methods of teaching reading to youngsters who are below grade level. Schools throughout the state of Iowa refer students, aged 10 to 13, to this program. It is very much like a summer camp, but the objective is to evaluate and improve reading ability. The young students stay in a dorm, visit edifying locations around the campus, go to school in a classroom like a typical elementary school, and attend sessions of group and individual reading instruction. The attendance is voluntary at a nominal cost to the families who enroll their child in this highly regarded opportunity.

Graduate and undergraduate students at the University of Iowa register in the Summer Reading Program as instructors of the young students to fulfill a degree requirement in several disciplines, such as a master's degree in special education. The university students must attend lectures in the mornings followed by small group discussions and planning in the afternoons. At some time in the afternoons, an individual session of reading instruction is conducted with the child that has been assigned to each of the university students. There have been introductory events in which the child and instructor get to know each other, such as observations of the child's classes and a group picnic. The individual sessions take place in a cubicle equipped with one-way glass and earphones for outside observation and listening. The monitors of these sessions are usually doctoral candidates that assist the professor in charge of the whole program.

Being involved with the University of Iowa's Summer Reading Program is a very pleasant and rewarding experience. This author attended the summer session facilitated by Dr. Linda G. Fielding, Ph.D. She is a very dedicated, hard-working, and personable professor of reading at the university's Education College. Dr. Fielding was very much involved with the monitoring of individual sessions with the children and guidance of the doctoral candidates that assisted her in the program. Lectures in the morning sessions were extremely interesting and first-rate. The knowledge and enthusiasm that Dr. Fielding exhibited in her subject was galvanizing.

The direction and characteristics of reading instruction took on the attributes of a religion. This assertion is not meant to be offensive or unkind. It was a very positive experience, but one had to adhere to the sacred texts in order to be accepted into the fold. One of the commandments was, "Thou shalt not speak the word that a child is trying to read." If a student was having difficulty reading a word, the instructor should guide the child to read the rest of the sentence, then go back and ask leading questions about the context of the sentence or pictures about the passage, but the child has to "read" the word. It was emphasized that any clues given should be about the concept of the whole word rather than phonetically presenting it, although hints as to "crunching" or breaking apart a word were acceptable as a last resort. If one were to stray from the correct practices, their transgression would be pointed out in the debriefing after the session was over.

The instructors that did embrace the true way were successful in the course. If the instructors felt threatened by the close monitoring of every move and continued to interject their own methodologies about reading, they became quite frustrated and were not as successful. They might have to undergo remedial instruction to get them on track. If that didn't work, excommunication may have resulted.

Of course, this tongue-in-cheek assessment of the Summer Reading Program is not meant to be pejorative. It is to point out that reading instruction in educational venues has become a flash point of discussions and beliefs. No one really understands why some children pick up reading well in the early grades and others do not. There is a wide spectrum of beliefs about how to teach reading, ranging from the discovery method to the total phonics approach. Those who employ the former usually produce middle schoolers who can't read, while those who subscribe to the latter have given sustenance to the commercial phonics industry.

In the discovery method, the idea is that kids will read when they are ready. In first and second grade, the teacher gives books to the students. Their inquisitive minds will want to discover what all those words and letters are about. So they will begin assigning meaning to words and discover a transcending higher plane, or "Zen" of understanding. The young minds will come to love reading as a magical process in which they discover more and more words, and they will grow up to be life-long lovers of reading. It frees the teacher from all those dreary phonics lessons so they may emphasize more important things like self-esteem. The trouble, however, is that the students have no idea how to attack a word for pronunciation by syllabification and letter/sound relationships. One of the doctoral candidates at the University of Iowa, who was teaching *Introduction to Learning Disabilities*, was no fan of this method. She related how her son once had a first grade teacher that went along with the school district's emphasis on this approach and bemoaned the fact that her son was now a sixth grader and essentially couldn't read.

In the other extreme, the emphasis is on phonics, phonics, phonics. Of the two—discovery or phonics—phonics is more benign. In phonics, there is drill upon drill of relating letters to sounds, rules, and single examples of each. It tends to produce slow readers and an association of reading to drudgery. It has been the experience of this author that sole emphasis on phonics produces poor spellers and writers. Their reading fluency is not markedly improved. For example, a student has been drilled to connect the "w" with rounding the lips to produce a sound so that when that child writes anything with a long "o", it is written as auto*w*mo*w*bile. Of course, in the case of *below*, it works. "Sow *what?*" you may ask. Well, you can see that it is phonics run rampant. It's what happens if there is a total emphasis on sounds at the expense of reading words as sight-words and using context clues in a sentence to discover words and meanings. It seems clear that the total phonics approach would take the joy out of reading. It also places a young learner in the untenable position of trying to spell sounds rather than words, especially difficult as English doesn't go by the rules of linguistics—unlike German, a language with no silent letters.

Why make reading so hard? Reading is best taught by incorporating different approaches and a variety of methodologies. Of course Johnny is not going to learn to read on his own. Of course there should be some phonics, but not all phonics. If the key to reading improvement were to be reduced to one word it would be "practice." Naturally, the more reading being done, the more Johnny will improve his reading. Remember, we're not going to make this hard. Word recognition ability is increased. Sight-word vocabulary increases, tremendously. Eye coordination across the page improves and phonetic patterns begin to register.

The main drawback of the conventional wisdom about not supplying a word for the struggling reader is that very few stories and books get read in a reasonable amount of time. Too much time is spent on a single word. Giving all the usual clues, such as "read to the end of the sentence and go back to the word," or "look at the picture," takes a lot of time. Reading instruction like this becomes no fun for the student because it emphasizes the struggle they are having with it. Reading should be for gaining knowledge or following a story for pleasure. How much fun would it be to watch a movie and have a public service announcement every couple of minutes? It's the same thing. The young, struggling reader becomes very "turned off" by the whole thing.

Now, you're in a classroom with 18 to 20 low readers. You are reading a story, together, aloud. A student is reading and comes to a word and says "machine" instead of saying the correct "mechanical." Don't make an issue of it. This was one of the many valuable lessons learned in the Summer Reading Program. Don't say anything. If he is reading along and says "cafeteria" instead of "capillary," correct the student right there in a gentle tone that is not judgmental. Give the student immediate feedback that may help register that word in a sight-word capacity. By the same token, give immediate feedback to the student who tackles and correctly reads a difficult word with a quick "great!" or "yes!" The notion in reading education that the reading instructor is supposed to be a disembodied entity that doesn't praise or correct is missing out on interaction opportunities. Praise is a powerful tool. It encourages effort and creates a pleasant and enjoyable atmosphere. Also, if you spend too much time getting one individual to arrive at a correct word, you are going to lose everybody else, and very few books are going to be read.

In the Summer Reading Program at the University of Iowa, many students showed no growth in reading skills. The student that this author tutored continued to read at the same level he had read during the previous summer. All of the conventional techniques were applied religiously. No growth was exhibited and the student could have read about four to five times the amount of 3rd grade level, picture books.

Reading is a complex issue. Granted, some readers have a definite reversal problem in their perception and it has a profound effect on their reading ability. Students with this puzzling disability are rare, but when they do appear in your classroom, their disability is obvious. I once had a student respond with the following letters when I asked him to spell "outdoors." He answered, "d-o-o-r-s-o-u-t." I don't have answers on how to deal with this except to help the child in ways that accommodate this condition, called "dyslexia" in medical terms. One thing is certain, the more the child read, the more he was able to accommodate his problem. What is the alternative? "I have dyslexia, so I shouldn't read"?

Here is a technique for involving low-functioning readers in reading. Students love to read aloud in the classroom if you have established a friendly and non-threatening atmosphere and a reward system is in place. Introduce a story by listing vocabulary words from the story on the overhead or chalkboard. To the right put definitions, out of order, so that the students must match up the words to the correct definition. Matching in small doses like this is good when it is a group project. Many teachers use a page-long matching technique for tests because they are easy to construct, but they overload a student with academic challenges. They become frustrated with all the data and end up bailing out by putting anything for their answers.

After matching the words to their definitions, cover them up or erase them. Introduce the story by asking some questions to pique class interest. For example, a story about sleepwalking could be introduced by asking if anyone has ever walked in his or her sleep. This will certainly engender some anecdotes about some adventures. In a short time, segue into the story by saying that this story is about a sleepwalker. Begin reading the story aloud. There will be plenty of volunteers to read. When the reader gets to one of the vocabulary words, whoever raises their hand first gets to identify the word and give a simple definition. If they were successful in saying something about the meaning of the word using their own words, a point should be awarded. There will be teachable moments as the story is read. Go with your instincts on occasion. If a phonics allusion is particularly appropriate, do it; just don't break the flow of the story too much. If checking for understanding seems appropriate by asking a couple of pertinent questions, by all means do that too. You, as the teacher, should read an occasional paragraph to keep things going. You will know when that is prudent. You will probably disappoint some students who wanted to read that paragraph that you decided to read. Believe me, you will have such enthusiasm in your class that there will be kids in contention about who can read next. Just have them follow the rules about raising hands quietly and be fair in choosing who is to read next.

Reading aloud is the only way to go when reading selections in a class of low readers. It keeps the students' attention, it accommodates slower and faster readers by keeping them together, it enhances word recognition, it promotes correct pronunciation, it heightens class participation, and it more positively ensures that that the pupils actually read the selection.

To review this reading methodology, as a student reads, gently say the word correctly if a word is misread or cannot be read by the reader. When difficult words are attempted and read correctly, exclaim a positive "great," or "good." Award points for reading aloud to any degree of success, just so reading is being done. Don't pause too much to teach phonics or other techniques because it detracts from the enjoyable flow of the story. That kind of teaching can be done at other times. With a room full of students, you won't lose their attention and you will read a lot of books and stories this way. When you finish a chapter or you arrive at a good stopping place, discussions about what has been read should be conducted utilizing the discussion techniques alluded to above. "Do you know how to get to Carnegie Hall?" a tourist asked a New Yorker. The New Yorker answered, "Practice, practice, practice!" Kids with reading problems become better readers the same way.

Lately, there has been a lot of attention paid to testing children in reading to see where their abilities lie. This is all well and good, but the way we have been teaching reading to low readers ensures that they will always score low on reading tests. In the old way, reading instruction is drudgery to the student with poor reading ability. To think that they would be happy to perform a reading test of 40 or 50 minutes and thereby establish an accurate reading level is very illogical. If you follow the methods put forth here, you can count on reading sessions being fun. It is fun both for the students and for the teacher. Furthermore, a lot of stories and books are being read. The drudgery index remains well within attentiveness parameters. After a year of this technique, students will be happy to perform a long reading test for you.

Chapter 4
The Journey to Better Writing Is an Ego Trip

The first week of language arts is devoted to writing the alphabet in cursive as an opening drill in a class period. The students should each have their own notebooks, which are actually wide-rule or college-rule spiral notebooks. Those with a marked writing difficulty should use the wider ruled, while most middle schoolers should use the college ruled. On an overhead projector, demonstrate the technique for writing the uppercase and the lowercase letters. Starting the letters and the direction one goes with the pen is important. Don't accept the "I can't write cursive" complaint. That is a non-sequitur. "I can't write cursive so I shouldn't practice cursive." If educators accepted that kind of logic our schools would be in a lot of trouble. Hey! We are in a lot of trouble. Tackle about six letters a day. Write a line of the cursive letters across the page. Walk around and look at the students' papers. Give positive input. I've never understood how a teacher could ask the students to get to work and never walk around to see how they are doing in order to offer encouragement and comments. A little "way to go" here and a few "looking good's" there makes a tremendous difference in the students buying in to what you are trying to accomplish.

How many of you teachers have ever heard, "I don't know what to write?" If it's not this complaint by one of your charges, it's one of a dozen other excuses to get out of writing. How about, "I don't have a pencil," (for this excuse, keep a box of golf pencils on hand—they're cheap) or "I didn't do anything over the week-end," or "I've never had a dream before"? It can be very exasperating. Well, here's a money-back guarantee. If you employ the techniques outlined in this chapter, and you don't produce avid and prolific writers, I'll give you back the price you paid for this book.

Most school districts have specific requirements with regard to writing. In middle school, the writing objectives in sixth grade center on writing several types of paragraphs. These are usually the descriptive, narrative, expository, and persuasive paragraphs. As the students progress through seventh and eighth grades, the expectations include multiple paragraphs and themes. Often, writing folders are created for the students' writing in sixth grade, in which more papers are added each year as they go on to high school and fulfill their writing requirements. Writing is an important skill. It is incumbent for every language arts teacher to figure out a way to get Judy or Johnny to write.

So, how do you get the recalcitrant writer to start turning some wheels and moving on from square one? With a room full of special education students—or general education students, for that matter—you've got to do something. Like most things in life that are valued, preparation is required. Sure, there are times that natural teachers are able to spontaneously carry a lesson through to a successful outcome. There are times when quick thinking produces the right response to a challenging situation that arises in a typical school day. These are valuable attributes that good teachers possess that are products of varying degrees of nature and nurture. It's what separates a great teacher from an amateur one. At the risk of being repetitively didactic—we've already had "practice, practice, practice"—here's a new adage: when asked to name three requirements necessary for being a good teacher, a veteran teacher answered, "Preparation. Preparation. Preparation."

Start with basics. Develop the construction materials necessary for building a paragraph. When school starts tell your charges that "neatness counts." The writing process is as much a function of aesthetics as it is for expressing thoughts and ideas. Look at some of the Asian cultures and how much they emphasize writing as an art form. Don't throw up your arms in defeat and say that some of your students have difficulty printing, writing, forming letters, and all manner of excuses for messy papers. Fine, then you've got your work cut out for you. You must start somewhere. If you have a student with a neuromuscular disorder, certain accommodations must be employed. I've had students who had to put a lot of effort into just forming letters, and uppercase mingled with lower case. They had no concept of spacing between words. Naturally, in a writing assignment, their goals were different from the rest of the class, but with each time they progressively showed growth and improvement. One technique that worked with the spacing was to put three little dots in-between each word and then erasing them later. They practiced the alphabet (just like everybody else) and learned to distinguish between upper and lower case letters. In a paragraph assignment, their goal was to write three sentences, not necessarily all at one sitting. The motivating techniques are illustrated later, but the point is every student is able to write something they can be proud of.

In a multi-categorical special education setting including students with learning disabilities, mental disabilities, and behavioral disabilities, most do not have neuromuscular dysfunction. Perhaps a real-world description of a typical self-contained special education classroom is in order here, especially to the uninitiated. A language arts class in special education may be from 15 to 23 students. The numbers seem to be growing because so many kids have difficulty with reading and writing. If someone were to walk into one of these classrooms, it would not appear to be any different from a general education language arts classroom. The reading book may contain easier reading material, perhaps three years behind grade level, but discussions and basic punctuation lessons could be very similar. There are probably a number of students who could do fairly well in the general education setting, but they need different motivational techniques and closer monitoring in order to survive in school. Most of the students in the class are able to write or print very neatly and legibly. They may exhibit quick thinking and be responsive in verbal interactions. In short, in the first two levels of more restrictive environments included in the 1.7 weight as outlined in the special education legislation, there are not a lot of observable differences between special education and general education. This is good, because students in this environment should not feel isolated or separated from the middle school setting. It's just another class that they attend.

Back to basics and teaching writing. Each student should have a spiral notebook for daily drills and writing practice. Keep them in the classroom to avoid the "I forgot my notebook" ploy for putting off work. Begin the year with filling pages by practicing the alphabet. Instill the idea of neatness and how a page of well-drafted letters looks pleasing to the eye. If a student balks at writing cursive, let him/her practice printing. It depends on the individual case. However, by middle school, the students should be writing cursive. Explain how cursive really helps their spacing in writing down words. It also becomes easier to write as the words flow onto the paper without having to lift a pencil all the time. You as the teacher will have to judge how much time to spend each day on practicing, as attention spans tend to be limited in special education, depending on the activity. Demonstrate on the overhead or chalkboard how to write in cursive, including starting points and directions. Do upper and lower case. The students will love it.

Some special educators think that writing on a word processor is a panacea for students who have difficulty writing. Yes, I think there is a place for writing on the computer. It may help students with spelling difficulties somewhat. Having computer skills classes is extremely valuable in the middle school curriculum. In classes such as those, practicing the writing process should be emphasized. It could be a life-long skill in these days of computer technology. But it shouldn't replace a physical writing skill that puts pen to paper. Is the student going to fill out applications on a word processor? Will the spell checker help or hinder the flow of creating a written work? It may be that words with a spelling similar to that of the intended word will continue to bring up red lines, or beep at the writer and hinder the creative flow of the writer. The writing of pen or pencil on a sheet of paper is like drawing a picture. Remember the glow of self-satisfaction on faces of the young child when presenting a completed drawing to someone he/she cares about? It can't be emphasized enough how correcting a rough draft with positive comments can mean so much in self-esteem. And then, wow, when the corrected copy is written and polished, you've really got something! At the same time in that step, a great deal is being learned by the student. Yes, it takes a lot of time for the teacher to read and correct, but it is vitally important.

So, you have worked on the building blocks of building a paragraph. Neatness has been encouraged and emphasized. Practicing the letters of the alphabet has been accomplished.. Differentiation of uppercase and lowercase letters has been learned. The next step is to practice writing a sentence. Make it simple. Insist only on starting a sentence with an uppercase letter and finishing with a period. Here is an effective drill. Tell the class you are going to write words or phrases on the chalkboard or overhead projector. The class is to write the word or phrase into a sentence. Write the word "dog." Walk around the room, checking for uppercase letters that start the sentence and periods that end it. If those criteria have been met, choose a person who has written a complete sentence to write it on the chalkboard or overhead. Chances are they will write, "I have a dog." for which praise is conferred. You now write, "has been running." Follow the same procedure around the room. A student might come up with, "Mary has been running around the track." The class will begin to get the idea of what a complete sentence is. And, they will find that they are quite capable of beginning a sentence with an uppercase letter and ending it with a period. Success produces success.

Do not cover parts of speech, subjects, complements, objects, predicates, and sentence structure at this time. The initial objective is to write ideas into sentences and sentences into paragraphs with a modicum of punctuation and spelling on a first draft. Nouns, verbs, adjectives, adverbs, and pronouns can be introduced as an ancillary activity to reading a story. I call this the "Mystery Word" activity. When a story has been read and discussed, it is fun to pick some word in the story as a mystery word. You will give the class five clues, one at a time, as to the word's identity. Make it a big deal by using colored construction paper on which you have written the clues prepared before hand. As you stick up the "Mystery Word" heading (with masking tape on the back), accompany it with a flourish and the all-important "ta da!" Now that you have the class' attention tell them that whoever can guess what the word is will get five points or some other form of recognition. However, if they guess too soon and therefore probably incorrectly, they are out of the game. (DQ'd – a term they understand). If you picked a noun, your first clue should be something like this: "The word is a noun. A noun names a person, place, or thing." This first clue provides an opportunity to name some nouns about the room. And, perhaps you may differentiate a proper noun from a common noun. The point is that each clue provides the teachable moment. The second clue is placed on the board: "It has three syllables." There follows a nice discussion about syllables. The third clue: "The second syllable has the short 'e' sound." This is a great opportunity for a little phonics discussion. The fourth clue could be, "One of these has days and numbers on it." The last clue could tell which page the word is on. By then, or perhaps before, someone has identified "calendar" as the mystery word. Throughout the course of the year, more difficult parts of speech and related language arts skills could be discussed in this manner.

We are ready to begin building our first paragraph. A short discussion of the types of paragraphs that the students will be expected to write over the course of a year would be useful at this time. Give a cursory description of descriptive, narrative, expository, and persuasive writing. Start with a descriptive paragraph. I have found that a description of their rooms at home is an excellent topic. Whether their room is in a corner of their basement or is a fabulous game room/bedroom, kids like to hang out in a place they call their own. They know it thoroughly, too. After all, they're the ones who hang posters in it, listen to the radio in it, watch TV in it, listen to CDs in it, get grounded in it, and maybe even do a little studying in it.

Ask the class to close their eyes and visualize their rooms in their mind's eye: What do you see? Raise your hands and tell me. As volunteers describe a fish tank, a poster, or a bed, write them down on the overhead projector or board. When this brainstorming produces a list, ask what these are about. What is the topic? Ah, it's about your room. Can you make a statement about your room? "I go to my room when I want to be alone." That, my little language arts friends, is a topic sentence.

At this time lay some groundwork on the basic structure of a paragraph. You have a topic sentence to introduce a subject or to tell the reader the paragraph's topic. The body of the paragraph contains supporting details or things about the topic that were brainstormed. A concluding sentence would wrap the paragraph up by restating the paragraph's topic, or bringing the paragraph to a close, and not leaving the reader hanging up in the air.

Perhaps we should give our creation a title. Notice the title shouldn't be done until the paragraph is complete. It should arouse interest. A reader will want to read on to find out what is meant by a title like, "My Secret Digs," or "Nintendo Nook," or "Poster Girl." The title is like a ribbon around the package or the frosting on the cake. It's an engaging finishing touch to a paragraph.

Before the students begin writing, emphasize the aesthetic look of their papers. Pass out a sheet of lined notebook paper for writing assignments. It ensures that everyone has the right kind of paper for his or her creation, and the uniformity of papers looks neater and more orderly in the writing files. On each one, put a pencil dot where the students are supposed to write their names, date, style of writing, where to indent, and title. On a final draft, the dots may be erased. Their papers should look a certain way so as to be pleasing to the eye. This aesthetic quality is instrumental in developing pride in their work. The students should also know what is expected. Demonstrate how their papers should look on an overhead projector or chalkboard as per below. Note the dot placement on each paper.

Aesthetics count in writing. Show students the correct format for their creation. Treat it like a work of art.

On the first few writing assignments, help the students with a topic sentence. Explain that topic sentences are statements that tell what the paragraph is about. Write down a few of their suggestions and a couple of your suggestions on the overhead and let the students choose one to begin their paragraphs. Encourage the students to write in short, powerful sentences. Be a minimalist when it comes to sentences. For example, in this particular assignment, "I like my room" would be an excellent beginning sentence. Another possibility is, "I have an interesting room." It shouldn't be any longer than, "I like to go to my room when I want to be alone." Students get started much more readily if they have help with a beginning sentence. Once the writing has begun, don't just sit at your desk correcting papers. Walk around the room and make positive comments about what you see. On occasion, pick up the paper of one that is formatted correctly, and the margins are maintained, and hold it up for the class to see. Make a comment of praise, such as, "James is really following directions." What's that you say? Not everyone is a neat writer? Aha! You don't have to be a neat writer or printer to have a neat paper. Any text looks neat when the paper is formatted correctly.

Now for the Rosetta stone, or key, for motivating reluctant writers to produce. Tell the class that at the end of the period you are going to read aloud some of the papers they have written without identifying the author. They have to guess who wrote the paragraph in three tries. The amount of interest this generates is astounding. The students love to hear their paper being read. The most obstinate student will quickly become a prolific writer when they see that in order to have something read they must produce. It may take one writing assignment to get this across. They might play the I-don't-know-what- to-write avoidance card once, but when their paper has not been read because they had only one or two sentences, they will be putting pencil to paper next time, rest assured.

Not only do kids like to have their own paper read aloud, there is a great deal of interest in trying to identify other writers. They will develop clever strategies for trying to identify who wrote what. Sometimes they look around the room to see who might be smiling, looking down modestly, looking proud, or possibly getting a little red, too. Another clue is not having a hand raised because no one would guess on his/her own paper. Of course, this little detail leads to a counter strategy of raising one's hand if your paper is being read to throw everybody off. At any rate, it is very gratifying to see the interest generated by this methodology. Of course, points could be awarded in different degrees, such as three points if you guess the author on the first try, for example.

Later in the year, there may be times when collecting papers that a student may whisper that they don't want their paper read aloud. This may be because of a sensitive subject in a narrative paragraph. Such requests, although rare, should be honored. Generally, it is a very enjoyable time for everyone as the class gets to know each other as the year progresses. They become adept at knowing who might be working on a go-cart engine, making cookies, playing basketball, or other little clues about their classmates. One time I was reading aloud from a stack of student logbooks. The class had requested that I read some of their answers to an essay question about a story we had read in order to "play the game." (I told you it was a popular activity). Anyway, after finishing this one selection, I looked up to see practically everyone's hand go up quietly without looking around at likely candidates. Turns out that the paper in this particular spiral notebook had distinctive light blue and white alternating lined paper and everyone could see whose notebook it was. We all had a good laugh about that.

WRITING STRATEGIES

Now that you have applied the motivation for writing, teaching the four main types of writing is important. In the first descriptive paragraph described above, helping the students with a topic sentence is very effective in getting the students to move off square one. After they have had some successful writing experiences, it is time to cover the four basic writing styles to fulfill the students' writing folders. In addition to descriptive writing, the students will be introduced to expository, narrative, and persuasive writing.

Expository. Expository means "to explain" or expose a topic to the light of day. It can be a "how to" writing assignment. It can be informational, perhaps on cause and effect relationships, as in how hail forms. Compare and contrast and book reviews are expository writing. Explaining how Abraham Lincoln came to be known as "Honest Abe," would be another example. For students in middle school who have difficulty writing, asking them to write a paragraph about how to make a peanut butter sandwich would be a crackerjack way to get the ball rolling in this kind of writing assignment. Start with a word bank. Ask the students to list words that would be used in making a peanut butter sandwich. Words like bread, butter, peanut butter, crunchy style, smooth, whole wheat bread, white bread, and knife should flow easily. Or how about action words like dip, extract, spread, cut, and place? When written on the overhead or board, these words will inspire the young writers to begin. Later, more substantive expository writing can be attempted.

Narrative. Narrative writing is telling a story, event or happening. One of its primary features is the sequence of events. It has a plot. It gives a setting, establishes conflicts, and introduces characters. It sets the stage, as it were. One way to teach this is to relate *The Three Little Pigs* story. It's a great example to start discussions about sequence of events. When the students are given their own topic, it is effective to have the students write down the sequence of events before starting to write the actual narrative. Also, *The Three Little Pigs* is a means to teach sentence variety, the use of vocabulary, and transition phrases, such as "after a time," "meanwhile," "first," "at the same time," "before this happened," instead of starting every sentence with "then," as the novice writer is apt to do. Narratives may be personal experiences or imagination. It may be written in the first or third person. A good first assignment is to ask the students to write childhood stories about something that happened, perhaps at a Thanksgiving dinner. At any rate, it's always easier for these kids to write about personal experiences. Maybe when they learned to ride a bike, or when their pet died, or a trick that backfired. A frightening experience, a day at the mall, or what they did last week-end. The point is to get them started. When you do the corrections, you can add a lot of instruction. As you do with a set of class papers, make a list of frequent errors. Go over those in class before you start them on their final draft.

Persuasive. Persuasive writing is designed to be convincing and assertive without the usual niceties of polite speech, such as, "In my opinion, we should have more control at what is being served in the cafeteria." Forget the "in my opinion." Tell your students to just go ahead and say that they should be empowered to pick lunch menus, if that happens to be a burning issue. When they make a statement about something they feel strongly, that is their topic sentence. To be convincing, the students should write about something they are involved with. Make the first assignment something that has a lot of ready facts and opinions which help them get started in brainstorming, such as making a web of ideas or just listing some facts. Webbing is not the end-all, be-all of writing. It's OK, but some kids do better with making a list. You could actually do brainstorming to come up with a topic. In persuasive writing, you can't really give them a topic. Students of this age often say they don't know what to write about, so open discussions of what's on their minds will help them pick a topic.

Chapter Five
Creative Ways to Teach Math

Despite what many perceive as a rebellious time in their development, students in middle school like order and structure in academic pursuits. Mathematics, by its very nature, is an excellent venue for providing concise expectations and the development of self-discipline. Your math class will be structured in such a way as to be captivating, stimulating, and user-friendly.

It is good to start off each math class with a game. One math game that has proved popular and enhances number sense is the in-between game. It's quite basic in that the student with the turn writes down a number between 1 and 1000 on a piece of paper to ensure that he doesn't change it as the game goes on. On the overhead or chalkboard, the student puts a 1 on the bottom and 1000 at the top. The class of players makes guesses as to the number. For example, say the secret number is 637. Someone guesses 858. The student who is performing the game says, "Too high," and places the 858 just under the 1000. Now the players have to guess between 858 and 1. After a few turns the game looks like this:

1000
858
800
750

10
5
1

The game is over when someone guesses the correct number. That person becomes the player to start the math class off the next day. There are all kinds of nuances about the game that one can employ, such as establishing the record guesses it took to arrive at the right number, usually around 17 tries. If a student makes a guess that cannot fit within the parameters, such as 760 in the game above, that student would be DQ'd (disqualified). By the way, special education students don't like to be patronized with little rules to make everybody like everybody else. If they're DQ'd, they're DQ'd. Those are the breaks of the game. It would be like playing baseball and saying you couldn't strike out. It just isn't reality. Be straightforward with your students. They will appreciate you for it.

Homework should be assigned every night, Monday through Thursday. On Fridays, tell the students that their assignment is to go out and have fun on the weekend, get dirty, and grow an inch, or whatever you can think of. Be creative! But, during the week they work. The usual lesson plan for each day is to play a short game such as the in-between game, correct the homework assignment, go over any questions, do some in-class thinking skills, such as story problems, give a new lesson, practice the lesson, and give the new assignment.

Many districts are reverting to various forms of the "new math" of the 70s in various camouflaged presentations. The result of that 70s adventure was to produce a majority of students who could not perform basic math problems of multiplication and division. Fractions were virtually left in the dust. The mathematicians feared that somewhere someone might be enjoying math in an understandable, practiced way. They were bogged down in arcane nomenclature. For a simple math question, instead of asking, "What number is ....," they would ask , "What is the integer that is the name of a real number on the whole number continuum that represents a positive value....blah, blah, ad nauseum."

Unfortunately, like so many periodic innovations in education, math is coming full circle. It may be packaged a little differently, and given purposeful direction, such as: it promotes more understanding, but the results are the same. Children who finish middle school should know how to add, subtract, multiply multi-digit numbers, do long division, and be competent with fractions. Most, however, are not able to perform these tasks adequately. However, it is safe to say that 99% of the young persons with a learning disability and a mild mental disability can perform addition and subtraction problems with a high degree of competency in middle school. This fact lends credence to the assertion that all the students, except for persons with a mental disability more pronounced than mild, could be able to perform practically every kind of mathematics computation found in the general middle school curriculum, given enough practice.

For the special education student, the direction he/she should go in mathematics is denoted in the IEP. Fortunately, there are enough similarities in your students' needs to be able to conduct a class and have them work on the same topic for your class lessons. Generally speaking, the middle school mathematics curriculum focuses on place value, rounding off, addition, subtraction, multiplication, division, decimals, fractions, geometry, story problems, and algebra. The following suggestions merely touch upon ways these disciplines might be taught for better understanding, practice, and enrichment.

PLACE VALUE, ROUNDING OFF, DECIMALS, and STORY PROBLEMS

Place value and rounding off go hand in hand. Start the year off with place value of whole numbers. Later, when addition, subtraction, multiplication, and division have been mastered, review place value and expand it into the place values of decimals. Using a variety of resources to impart understanding of place value has proven helpful. Some textbooks do a good job of making colorful displays of the value hierarchy. Use poker chips that have been colored (by markers) to represent different values. For example, a purple poker chip is worth 10 blue chips, and a blue chip is worth 10 red ones, and so on. These can be hands-on manipulatives to "play" with and visualize the concept.

When decimals are addressed, having an overhead transparency with squares divided into 100 little boxes like graph paper is advisable.

One whole square (enclosing 10-by-10 little squares) represents the whole number one. Each little box is one hundredth, or one column is one tenth. It's a good way to demonstrate "the land of less than one." Those are the numbers to the right of the decimal. Fill in a couple of little boxes and you've got .02. Fill in 35 little boxes and you've got .35. The homework assignment after this lesson could be a page of these graphs with a decimal written underneath and the students have to fill in the correct amount of little boxes.

Act place value out. Put a big round black dot on the wall and adopt a tone of voice like George Carlin's and say, "I'm standing in the land of whole numbers. I could keep walking that way and the numbers would get bigger and bigger." Now walk to the other side of the dot and say, "Now I'm in the land of less than 1. If I kept walking that way [pointing], the numbers would get smaller and smaller." You can expand this theme to include taped place values on the floor at which kids could stand to represent different place values. You get the picture.

When rounding off, knowledge of place value is essential. Say you are going to round off 34.768 to the nearest tenth. Write the number on the board. Go up to the 7, underline it, and say "7, you're either going to stay the same or go up one. I'll get back to you." Now look to the number to its right and say, "6, you and everything to your right are going to disappear. I just wanted to see if you were bigger than a 4." Erase the 6 and 8 and turn back to the 7 and say, "The one on your right was bigger than a 4 so you go up one. Everything to your left stays the same." Change the 7 to an 8 so that 34.8 is left. If the number to the right of the underlined number is less than 5, the underlined number stays the same. This procedure works for any number that is rounded off—whole numbers or decimals. It is fun to act things out and the students really pay attention when their teacher is going up to a number and talking to it. Always start by underlining the number in the place to which the number is being rounded off.

There is one modification that is necessary to the rule above. If you are rounding off to the nearest tenth (or any place), and the place is occupied by a 9. You go through the above procedure, and the number to its right is bigger than a 4, so you tell the 9 that it's going to be a 10. Start to write the 10 down in that place and say, "Oops. The 0 tells the 1 that there's not room for both of them. The 1 has to add itself to the next number up." Of course, if the number to the right of the 9 is less than 5, the 9 stays the same.

As one introduces decimals, it is important to get the terminology mastered. When reading a number such as 424.768, the students should be able to say "four hundred twenty-four and seven hundred sixty-eight thousandths." The main point is that they say "and" for the decimal point, and, wherever the number ends, that's the place that is spoken. Since the 8 is in the thousandths place, after the "and" for the decimal, you read the number six hundred sixty-eight thousandths. If the number were .76, you would say, "seventy-six hundredths."

Following the introductions of decimals over one to two weeks, move into adding and subtracting numbers that contain decimals, including money. This is not difficult as the decimals in an addition and subtraction algorithm go straight down into the addend and difference. If gathering numbers to add or subtract, ensure that the decimals are lined up. Proceed at own pace, incorporating story problems in which the students have input as to the data when practicing these kinds of problems. You might ask, "Who would like to go to the _________ store?" (Name a local store where one can buy video games, CD's, or clothes. The students really tune in to this sort of involvement). Ask the volunteer what he/she would buy. Write down what it would cost. Then ask someone else the same question. Write down what he or she would spend. From there, ask how much did they spend in all? Or, how much more did Mary spend than Isaac? Naturally they need to line up the numbers so that the decimals are in line. This is a good time to discuss key words that are clues to the processes that are required to solve problems.

Special education children have a difficult time with story problems. They usually make a wild guess on whether to add some numbers in the problem, or subtract them. Like a lot of things, practicing will improve their performance. At this stage, concentrate on addition and subtraction. Teach key words that will give them a clue, such as "**in all**," for addition. For subtraction, "**more** or **more.... than**," as in, "how much **more** did Zach spend **than** Justin?" Multiplication is just an quicker way to add. If there were 4 trees and each tree had 2 squirrels, how many squirrels were there **in all**, which is either addition or multiplication. Later on, when working with division, introduce some key word for division. If a question has "**each**" in it, it's probably a division problem. For example, 60 students went on a field trip. Parents were driving 5 vans. How many kids would there be in **each** van? See, division: 60 ÷ 5 = 12 kids in each van.

Of course, the students must throw out unrelated facts. On some problems, put in something completely unrelated to help them think about what is necessary to solve a problem. Here is an example: An airport had 72 flights take off every day. Each plane carried 75 people. By noon, one day, 37 flights had taken off. How many more flights were left that day? This, of course, is a subtraction problem that has nothing to do with the 75 people per plane.

As story problems are developed for in-class work, award points for successful completion of a problem. Make them "three pointers" as you walk around the room looking at answers. As mentioned before, assign someone to be scorekeeper on a score sheet with everyone's name on it. From that tally put the points on the official score sheet on the wall. As you walk about, point to a correct answerer like a wrestling referee and say with three fingers held aloft, "Three points," which the score keeper will dutifully record. If the student has attempted something and made a mistake, offer encouragement and guidance so that they will arrive at the answer and reduce the score to two or one points. Be honest in relationships to your pupils. Students don't appreciate being talked down to nor being awarded points that are not earned.

Working on thinking skills as described above can be done in a wide variety of subjects. Of course it's a lot of work to be prepared, but preparation and variety is what makes it work. The latter part of the class time should be devoted to skills of computation that set up the evening's homework. Students like homework if it is clear, valid, rewarded, and carries a high degree of expected success, the latter being crucial to any kind of motivation. If addition of decimals is the present unit, assign 10 problems of adding numbers with decimals after class time has been partitioned to doing some like algorithms and checking for understanding. Remember to assign homework every night except Friday when you assign them to go and have fun over the weekend.

MULTIPLICATION

Sure, you should explain what multiplication is and why it works, but rote practicing is how students learn to do it. Do special education kids understand it? Yes, they do, to the degree that it will get them accepted into a school or will help get them a job.

When practicing algorithms, or problems, talk to the numbers. When you are multiplying 5 times 435, say, "The five goes '5 times 5 is 25.'" You start to write the 25 down below and you stop and say, "The 5 says, 'hey, wait a minute 2, you can't come down here. There's only room for me. You gotta go up above the next number that is being multiplied, the 3. You're being carried, 2, above the 3.' 'Oh, OK,' says the 2. And you write the 2 above the 3. "Now you've got to take the 5 times the 3, which is 15." You start to write down 15 and you say, "Now the 2 is ticked. First he got sent up here and now nobody is paying any attention to him. So the 2 says, 'Hey, what about me?' You're right 2, we gotta add you to the 15 to make 17." You start to write down the 17 and you say, "The 7 says to the 1, you can't come down here. There's only room for me. You gotta go above the next number. You gotta carry yourself up above the next number—the 4." And so it goes. It makes it enjoyable for the students to see and hear this little drama every time you multiply some numbers. It helps them visualize and "get" multiplication.

When doing more complex multiplication with 2-digit multipliers, it is helpful to draw blank lines below where the products are going to be placed. Like this:

$$
\begin{array}{r}
328 \\
\times 34 \\
\hline
\_\ \_\ \_\ \_ \\
+\quad \_\ \_\ \_\ \_ \\
\hline
\_\ \_\ \_\ \_\ \_
\end{array}
$$

When teaching 2-digit multiplication, explain that when you multiply the top factor by the second lower factor, the 3 in the above example, you are really multiplying by 30. So, always start the *first* "extra" line with one zero. Then finish the line with the usual multiplication. It is important that they do this automatically as they practice, practice, practice. When you move to multiplying with 3-digit factors, you would say that on the *second* extra line put two 0's starting on the right.

DIVISION

To prepare your math class for long division, place brightly colored posters around the room that say nothing more than:

DIVIDE
MULTIPLY
SUBTRACT
BRING DOWN

When you actually begin to teach long division, start with simple problems like $8\overline{)64}$. Don't just say that 8 is the answer. Start by covering up the 4 in the dividend and asking, "Does a group of 8 people fit in a 6-seat van?" No of course not. When the class answers with a collective "No," say, "Well put an x over the 6 then, because it doesn't compute." Pull back your hand, revealing the whole 64, and ask, "Does a group of 8 people fit on a 64-seat bus?" They will give an affirmative response. Then ask, "How many groups of 8 can you get on a 64 passenger bus?" Some will get it right away, knowing that $8 \times 8 = 64$, thereby saying 8 groups will fit on the bus. It is crucial at this time to demonstrate that for the slower processors so that they can visualize the division concept. Draw a bus with 64 seats (or have one ready) and count and show how many groups of 8 the 64-seat bus could accommodate.

After 8 has been shown to be the correct answer,

$$\begin{array}{r} \times\ 8 \\ 8\overline{)\,6\ 4} \\ \underline{6\ 4} \end{array}$$

or the quotient, place the 8 next to the x and above the 4. Tell the class that we have just divided and that is where the answer goes. Then ask, "Are we done?" as you point to the posters around the room. "What do we do after we divide? Right. We multiply." Multiply 8 times 8 and write the 64 below the 64 in the dividend. Continue asking the question, "Are we done? No, the poster says subtract, so subtract. There's nothing there. You could put 0s there, but it isn't necessary. 'Bring down' is next. If there is nothing to bring down, you're done." Go over and over this. Practice. Practice. Practice. There is nothing wrong with rote learning once you have explained why and how something works. There is a place for both thinking skills and drills in mathematics.

Sometimes, starting off with division, special education students just don't get the concept of "goes into," This term, come to think of it, is probably anathema to mathematicians. Hogwash! Math coordinators of school systems or other math gurus keep trying to make changes in math curriculum. Are they just trying to promote themselves and give meaning to their existence? There are commercial enterprises lining up to accommodate them and sell their products. Textbook publishers are very good at creating needs where one doesn't exist. They will suggest to school systems that old textbooks do not teach students how to think. They get these ideas from mathematicians in academia that are in their employ. The mathematicians' mantra is "abstract thinking good, rote drill bad." The "discovery" approach to math may be good for a few students, but frustrated students and parents are legion. We went through this in the '60s and '70s. It was called "New Math," which produced a generation of students who couldn't do the most basic computations.

At any rate, there is a way to get across the concept of "goes into" to a math student who is struggling with division. Take 57 ÷ 8. You've already done the "how many 8's in 57?" bit, and the "what times 8 equals a number close to 57?" query to no avail. So, you say, " Suppose you are going to a restaurant and you are in a group of 8. You go up to the *maitre d' hotel* and say, ' do you have room for a party of eight?' And he says, "Of course we do. We have 57 empty seats, so we have room for 7 parties of 8 and 1 seat left over.'" Your students will understand this with amazing clarity.

Here's another technique when introducing division. This really helps the students to grasp the concept. If you have 21 ÷ 7 = ? You could put 21 little marks on the paper. Then, begin drawing a circle around groups of seven. How many groups of 7 can you find? 3? Yes!

FRACTIONS

Fractions have been a problem for special education students, and even for general education students. Why? It's probably because of how fractions are taught. A lot of teachers start by going over the terminology: This is a numerator. This is a denominator. This is a mixed number. This is an improper fraction. They tell how to do something, give an assignment, and expect all of them to get it. It doesn't work that way, certainly not with marginal students. Sure, some of the bright ones with left-brained facility in number concepts may take to fractions easily. Most of the students, though, benefit from strategies and drills that imbed the concepts within their frame of reference and understanding.

Sometimes purchased textbooks or programs can be an impediment to universal mastery. In some of the more hierarchical, affluent school districts with levels of administration that include mathematics coordinators, the teachers in the school buildings have to pay homage to the math curriculum *du jour*. What does this mean? It means that a central administration office has purchased a mathematics program and/or concomitant textbooks from a salesman that has been generous with budgeted sales largess. The new math program may be a lot of eyewash that looks attractive and interesting to kids. One purchased math program has two weeks spent on working in groups of four, cutting out strips of paper, dividing them into parts and making consensus decisions on what equivalent fractions are. The phrase "lowest terms" is completely foreign to the students.

A sure-fire way to introduce fractions is to buy a few of those flat, 1.55-ounce, Hershey chocolate candy bars. These rectangular candy bars are marked off into 4 columns of 3 little rectangles, or 12 little sections. Start the class by unwrapping one of these candy bars and asking the class if they would rather have ½, ¼, or 1/12 of this candy bar. You will have their attention. Some may go for the fraction with the number 12 in it because it is bigger. When they think about it, ½ may not be all that bad. After they have thought about it for a moment, ask someone to count all the little squares. Yes, there are 12 of them. Break one off and say that it is one-twelfth. Break off another section of 6 and show one-half of the candy bar. Say, "Now which would you like, one-twelfth or one-half?"

There are a lot of directions you can go with the candy bar lesson. Show that one-half of the candy bar is six-twelfths, or two-fourths, or, of course, one-half to initiate a discussion about equivalent fractions, and, yes, even *lowest terms.* Introduction of the *numerator* and *denominator* is possible in this scenario, too. Write that the numerator tells the number of pieces, or how many pieces. Call it NUMBERator if you have to, just so they know the concept. The denominator tells the denomination or kind of group we are talking about. "Are we talking twelfths here, halves, fourths, or what? Tell me." Look at the candy bar (or a diagram of same) and find all the different kinds of groups you can make out. For example, you can see the three rows. They represent the denominator of thirds. Two rows equal two thirds. Hey, look. Three thirds is the same as one whole. You can have a lot of fun with it. The enthusiasm of the teacher cannot be stressed enough as the champion of motivational techniques.

It is suggested that the first assignment for homework be variations on the Hershey's candy bar theme. Have a facsimile of the candy bar drawn on a worksheet. Embolden the lines that divide the candy bar into sixths. Underneath write, "Color four-sixths." In another diagram embolden the lines that put the candy bar into fourths. Likewise, direct the student to shade in ¾. Devise a worksheet that has a lot of these for coloring and you've got your assignment for the night.

As you progress in fractions, there have to be some nuts and bolts type of rote learning. You can explain why things work the way they do, but they still have to practice a lesson many times to get it down. Take adding fractions. Sure, adding fractions of like denominators is quite understandable and easy to perform. You show the proverbial pie cut into 8 pieces. What is one-eighth plus three-eighths? Four-eighths, right? What's another name for four-eighths? Right! One-half. You've got it.

Let's talk about adding fractions that have different denominators. They must be the same category or have the same denominator in order to add them, or subtract, for that matter. When adding three-fourths plus one-third, one must re-name them so that they will have the same denominator. This is called finding equivalent fractions that have the same denominator. Ask for ideas. Guide them to think of the candy bar. It should be discovered that three-fourths is the same as nine-twelfths and one-third is the same as four-twelfths. *Voila!* You have got the same denominator for both addends.

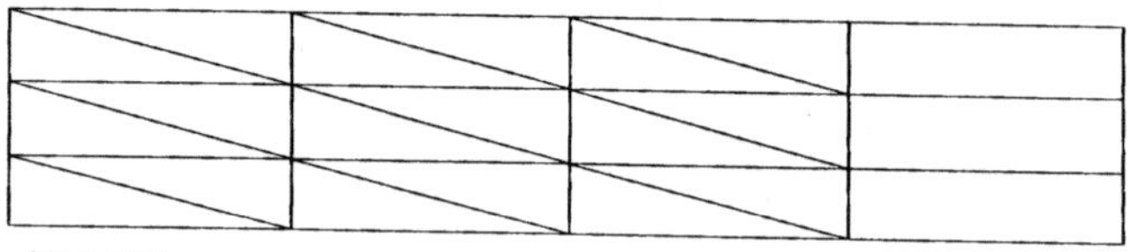

3/4 = 9/12

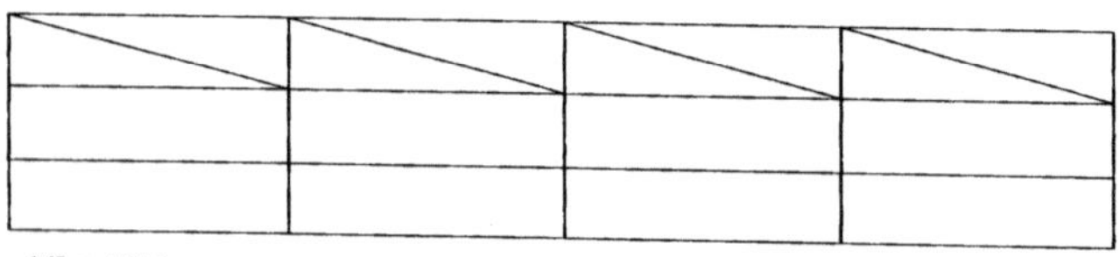

1/3 = 4/12

Nine-twelfths plus four-twelfths equals thirteen-twelfths. How many twelfths made one candy bar? Right. Twelve. So, this makes one candy bar and one-twelfth more. This is the moment to make a tangent into improper fractions (larger numerator than denominator) and renaming them into mixed numbers (or whole numbers).

It is understood in mathematics that anytime there is a number over another number, such as 13/12, it means to take the under number into the over number, if you want to write it in a different way. 13 divided by 12 equals 1 and a remainder of 1/12. Or, one can re-write any fraction into a decimal in this way, such that 13/12 also equals 1.08333, but that's a different story. We are talking about fractions here. So, tell your students that anytime you have a fraction, in which the numerator is bigger than the denominator, divide the denominator into the numerator to get a mixed numeral. Whatever you have as a remainder goes over what you are dividing by. Example: 7/4. 4 goes into 7 once with 3 left over. Therefore, 7/4 = 1 ¾. Sometimes there is nothing left over, like in 8/4 = just 2.

So, in teaching fractions there are: proper fractions (when the numerator is smaller than the denominator, like 3/4), improper fractions (when the numerator is bigger than the denominator, like 6/5), and whole numbers (a whole number by itself, like 2, or any number over 1, like 2/1, or 8/4).

In the real world, how should kids practice adding and subtracting a whole bunch of fractions? First, find a common denominator. That is, when adding 2/3 + 5/8, put them over and under like below. What bigger numbers will both 3 and 8 go into evenly? Or better yet, what are the multiples of 3 and 8? Explain that when you list multiples, you are really counting by that number. So, count by 3s: 3, 6, 9, 12, 15, 18, 21, 24, 27, 30. List these on a piece of scratch paper. Say that counting up to 10 numbers is good. Now, list the multiples of 8, and we are looking for a match to the multiples of 3: let's see, multiples of 8: 8, 16, 24, 32.... Wait. We've got a match! It's 24. 24 is the smallest match. We go for the smallest match. So now put 24 as the denominator in both problems.

$$\frac{2}{3} = \frac{\quad}{24}$$

$$+\ \frac{5}{8} = \frac{\quad}{24}$$

And now for the mark of Zorro! In this case, the Z goes from the bottom up. In the top addend, draw a line from the 3 to the 24 and say, "3 goes into 24, 8 times. 8 times 2 (drawing the diagonal to the 2) is 16 (draw the top of the Z to the blank)." Do the same thing to the bottom addend: "8 into 24 is 3. 3 times 5 is 15." You have just written equivalent fractions for the two original addends that now have like denominators. Now adding is no problem. Sixteen twenty-fourths plus fifteen twenty-fourths is thirty-one twenty-fourths. 31/24 is an improper fraction. 24 goes into 31 one time and 7 twenty-fourths left over. The final answer: 1 and 7/24.

Some math classes of the new, new math spend weeks teaching the concept of equivalent fractions by making a number line and dividing it into fractions. Where the lines are the same, you have equivalent fractions, such as 2/3 and 8/12. Perhaps one should spend one lesson on that concept and then teach the students something they can quickly work with, like converting two addends to equivalent fractions that have the same denominator. That they can use. To reiterate: list multiples of each denominator. Find the lowest common multiple (LCM). Divide the LCM into the denominators, take that number times the numerator, and put the results as the new numerator.

Reducing Fractions to Lowest Terms

Reducing fractions to lowest terms is very important to learn when studying fractions. It doesn't have to be emphasized right away. Let the students learn how to add fractions, first. Then emphasize the need to convert fractions to lowest terms, when necessary.

You may recall that adding fractions required that the student list multiples of denominators until there was a match when adding unlike fractions. Listing factors of the numerator and denominator helps converting fractions to lowest terms. Factors are all the combination of numbers that when multiplied equal a number. The factors of 8 are 1, 8, 2, 4. Every number has at least two factors, one and itself. A number that has only 2 factors, like 17 (1,17) is called a prime number. In a fraction 8/12, the factors of 8 are 1,8, 2,4, and the factors of 12 are 1, 12, 2, 6, 3, 4. Find the greatest common factor (GCF) and you see 4. Once that is established, divide 4 into both the numerator and the denominator and you have the lowest terms of 2/3. If the GCF is 1, then the fraction is already in lowest terms. The special education classes may need a multiplication table to accomplish some of these tasks.

There are little tricks to tell your students when reducing fractions to lowest terms. They will need all the help they can get because lowest terms are very difficult for the special needs student to accomplish. Whenever the numerator is the same as the denominator, it equals 1. Whenever the denominator is twice as big as the numerator, it equals ½. If there are 0's on both the numerator and the denominator, cancel them out, i.e., if you cross out the zero on a numerator, you must do the same on the denominator. In other words, divide both by 10. If you have 20/30, it is easily reduced to 2/3 with this method.

The latter "trick" is a perfect example of how math coordinators in a school district, or so-called experts of mathematics pedagogy, would cringe at "just cancel out the 0's." That is the easiest way for students to reduce fractions in a case like that. The old "new" math proponents and the new, "new" math proponents would say no, no, no! You must pull out your paper strip that has been divided into 30ths that you have been working on, if you still have it. If not, make another paper strip divided into little marks representing 30ths. Count up to 20 little marks. Does this mark have an equal spot on some of the larger segments of 0 to 1 number strips; say one that has been divided into thirds? Good. It looks like 2/3, doesn't it? In the meantime, we could be a lot farther in the practice of reducing to lowest terms.

There must be a lot of practice, practice, and practice to master the techniques and understanding in fractions, and general mathematics, for that matter. That's why we have homework assignments every night. Keep the parents apprised of your homework schedule (every night, but not on the weekends). It is a wonderful opportunity for parents or caregivers to work with their child, especially when math is presented in such a way that they understand it. Help at home is a good thing. There are several instances in which a parent has become closer to the child because of this opportunity to work together. As has been stated here before, the continuity of drill and practice assists the students' mastery of certain math skills. Students should be told to wrestle their math problems. Grapple with them. Fight the good fight until you beat them and pin them. Get animated with this. Your enthusiasm is catching when you act out wrestling the pesky math problems as a little pep talk when you give the assignment.

Another way to reduce fractions employs the multiplication chart. Students are familiar with this tool for multiplying and dividing, so they should be able to grab onto this technique rather easily and will be amazed at how quickly they can reduce fractions. Observe the multiplication chart below. Pick any fraction, such as 12/16. Start on the furthest right column, the one headed by 9, and draw your finger down the column looking for a 12 and 16 in that same column. Nope. There isn't a 12 *and* 16 in that column. Now, move to the left to the column headed by 8. Is there a 12 and 16 in that column? There is a 16, but not a 12. So you move one column to the left. Keep going until you find 12 and 16 in the same column. In the 4 column you have a 12 and 16. Now that you have located them, draw your finger to the left from the 12 all the way and you land on 3. Do the same from the 16 and you land on 4. So, 12/16 reduced to lowest terms is 3/4. It's that easy. Of course, you are basically finding the largest common factor of the 12 and 16, which is 4, and dividing both by 4 to get 3/4. But, if the chart helps a student reduce fractions, encourage the use of it.

X	1	2	3	4	5	6	7	8	9
1	1	2	3	4	5	6	7	8	9
2	2	4	6	8	10	12	14	16	18
3	3	6	9	12	15	18	21	24	27
4	4	8	12	16	20	24	28	32	36
5	5	10	15	20	25	30	35	40	45
6	6	12	18	24	30	36	42	48	54
7	7	14	21	28	35	42	49	56	63
8	8	16	24	32	40	48	56	64	72
9	9	18	27	36	45	54	63	72	81

Determining Relative Size of Fractions

Mastery of fractions would include the ability to put unlike fractions into size order. Given two fractions, such as 4/11 and 3/8, which is biggest? One could find a common denominator and determine relative size that way. The smallest common denominator, that is a number that is divisible by 8 and 11, is 88. Hence the first fraction is 32/88, determined by 11 into 88 goes 8 times. 8 times the numerator 4 is 32, or 32/88. The second fraction determined the same way is 33/88. So, the larger of the two fractions is 3/8.

Using a calculator to quickly divide the numerator by the denominator will easily tell which fraction is largest, too.

Another way is using lines that represent the whole number 1. Divide those into parts of the fractions in questions. Thus 11ths looks like this: (As when the students do this, it doesn't have to be perfect).

```
I--------I--------I--------I--------I-------I-------I--------I--------I--------I--------I--------I-------I
          1/11     2/11     3/11      4/11    5/11   6/11     7/11     8/11     9/11     10/11
```

The 8ths line looks like this:

```
I-----------I-----------I-----------I-----------I-----------I-----------I-----------I-----------I
           1/8         2/8         3/8         4/8         5/8         6/8         7/8
```

One can observe that it is hard to tell which is farthest along the number line, so it has its drawbacks. If a semblance of accuracy is maintained when drawing the number line, this is an effective way to picture fractions in the mind's eye of the young learner. The number line may also be used to talk about equivalent fractions. If the 8ths line could be placed under a 4ths line, the student could visualize that 2/8 is the same as 1/4, and likewise 6/8 to 3/4.

The number line technique is a useful tool when determining the size of several fractions, such as 3/6, 1/8, 5/12, and 2/3. Putting them in order from smallest to largest is the task. Mathematically, finding the least common denominator (24) and working it out that from smallest to largest they are: 1/8, 5/12, 3/6, and 16/24. Making 4 number lines and dividing them into the parts indicated is a hands-on exercise that slowly reveals the relative sizes.

Multiplying Fractions

Talk about getting animated. The following cheer will get your class' attention. It's from Dr. Larry Leutzinger of the University of Northern Iowa. You can make up your own choreography:

Multiplying fractions
That's no problem
Take the top times the top
And the bottom times the bottom

What more can be said? Write fraction multiplication problems laterally: $1/2 \times 1/4 = 1/8$. It's quite simple to multiply fractions. As the verse indicated, just multiply the numerators times the numerators. You must also multiply the denominators times the denominators. It isn't necessary to have common denominators, as in addition or subtraction. When multiplying the top times the top and the bottom times the bottom, the most difficult part will be for the students to convert answers to lowest terms if applicable. There is a short cut to multiplying fractions, called canceling, that helps to make the product less unwieldy and more conducive to rewriting to lowest terms or, if need be, mixed numerals.

Canceling cannot be done in every multiplication problem, but may be done when there are common factors in a cross juxtaposition of numerator of one fraction to the denominator of the other fraction that is being multiplied. In the algorithm 5/24 × 8/35, below, find the common factor in 5 and 35 and divide both by it. You've got it. It's 5. How many groups of 5 are in 5, or 5 goes into 5 how many times? The answer to both forms of the same question is, of course, 1. So, cancel out the 5 in the numerator of the first fraction and replace it with 1. How many groups of 5 are in 35, or 5 times what equals 35, or how many times does 5 go into 35? Right! It's 7, so cross out the 35 and write in 7. How about the other numerator and denominator in our crossing pattern? Yes, the 24 and the 8 have a common factor, the largest being 8. Do the same procedure and you have replaced the 8 with a 1 and the 24 with a 3. Now, the problem reads 1/3 × 1/7 for a product of 1/21, which is much easier for the young math students to have to deal with than 40/840.

$$\frac{\overset{1}{\cancel{5}}}{\underset{3}{\cancel{24}}} \times \frac{\overset{1}{\cancel{8}}}{\underset{7}{\cancel{35}}} = \frac{1}{21}$$

Dividing Fractions

Dr. Leutzinger has a verse for dividing fractions, too, with cartwheels and ending with arms and legs in a big X .

Dividing fractions
That's our cry.
Invert the second one
And then you multiply

Why does that work? It seems so simple, but why does dividing fractions work by the old "invert and multiply?" It will only work by inverting the divisor, which is the second fraction. If you invert the first fraction you will get a wrong answer.

If you had an equation like this:

$$1/2 \div 1/4 =$$

You are saying, "How many 1/4s are in 1/2?" We can visualize this by thinking of a ruler. There are two 1/4s in 1/2 inch. That is common sense.

Mathematically, following the rule of inverting the second fraction and multiplying, you have:

$$1/2 \times 4/1 = 4/2 = 2$$

Perhaps the "why" of inverting and multiplying can be demonstrated with an algorithm like this:

$$6\overline{)18}$$

This is the same as

$$18 \div 6 \text{ . Or, } \frac{18}{1} \div \frac{6}{1}$$

Invert the divisor to 1/6 and change the sign to × and you have

$$\frac{18}{1} \times \frac{1}{6},$$

which is the same as 1/6 of 18 is 3 or 1/6 × 18 = 3.

Go ahead and explain why one inverts and multiplies to divide fractions. Then, just do it and practice it. There won't be any of your students' parents complaining that their kids aren't learning the basics in math.

GEOMETRY

The scope of this book, of course, is not intended to cover theory and depth of a subject, but to share techniques for presenting and capturing students' attention. The focus here is on plane geometry, rather than solid geometry. The former is one-dimensional, limited to "flatland" in which there is length and width, but no depth. The latter is three-dimensional—length, width, and depth. A circle in plane geometry may present problems for finding a circumference, diameter, radius, and area. In solid geometry, a circle may be expanded to a cylinder, a square a cube, a triangle a cone, etc. Volume comes into play. In a middle school introduction of geometry, plane geometry will be a sufficient challenge.

Introducing Geometry

Geometry affords a good deal of hands-on motor skills with tools that are fun to use. Prior to getting out compasses, rulers, and protractors, invite the students to identify geometric figures all around them. Talk about squares, rectangles, triangles, circles, pentagons, octagons and what they are. Then, look around. Can you see some of these shapes in our everyday world? Hey, is the window a rectangle or a square? This may lead to a discussion on the difference between a square and a rectangle. Look outside. See that stop sign? Do you know what shape that is? An octagon? Right! There could easily be 20 minutes spent on a discussion of the various shapes and their definitions. Getting out rulers and pencils, drawing some figures of choice, and labeling them should follow this. Merely becoming familiar with using a ruler to draw a straight line is the lesson for the day. The homework assignment for the night should be to draw figures to specifications, such as "draw a square that has 3 inches to a side." Other tasks could be to draw a rectangle that is 2 inches by 4 inches, draw one triangle that has a square corner, and draw any shape that has five sides.

When you correct the assignment tomorrow, begin to talk about angles. A square corner has 90 degrees. What are degrees? There is your lesson for the day. Put a dot on the board or overhead projector. This is a point. Draw a line. This is a line. Draw the line at a funny angle, i.e. not straight across or up and down. Put a ruler on the line. Move the ruler a notch from the line, keeping it touching the line at one end so that it has formed a small angle. This is a degree. Move it again. This is another degree. Keep it moving, forming a larger and larger angle until there is a right angle. This is 90 degrees, or a "right" angle. Then continue with this approach until you have gone all the way to 180 degrees, or a straight line.

Now it is time to get out the protractors. The major problem with the young learner and angles is they don't know which number to read when making or reading angles. Start off by talking about square angles of 90 degrees. Anything sharper than that angle is an acute angle and would be less than 90. Anything more than a square corner is an obtuse angle and would be greater than 90. Still, many students will put a protractor down on a fairly sharp angle and read the first number they see and say that it is 160 degrees when it really is only 20 degrees! They should apply thinking skills before making a quick judgment to please. But that's OK. Errors of enthusiasm are much preferred over errors of apathy.

Nevertheless, despite instruction and logic that an angle sharper than a square corner will be less than 90 degrees, students will still put the protractor on an angle and read "160." Back to the drawing board! Yes, it certainly does look like 160 degrees, but more instruction is needed. Let's measure 120 degree angle. Place the little mark in the center of the protractor on the point of the angle, and position one of the 0's on one of the lines of the angle. Now, starting with the 0, start counting up from that until you reach the other ray of the angle. The number you count to is the degree of that angle. OK. Here's the zero on the line. Now, let's see. The first number as I count up is 10, 20, 30, 40, 50, 60, 70, 80, 90, uh...what comes after 90, oh yes, 100—there it is. So, moving along, I come to the other ray of the angle and it's right on the 120. There it is, 120 degrees. It's not the 60 because it's greater than a square corner (90), and you start with one side of the angle and count up until you get to the other side of the angle.

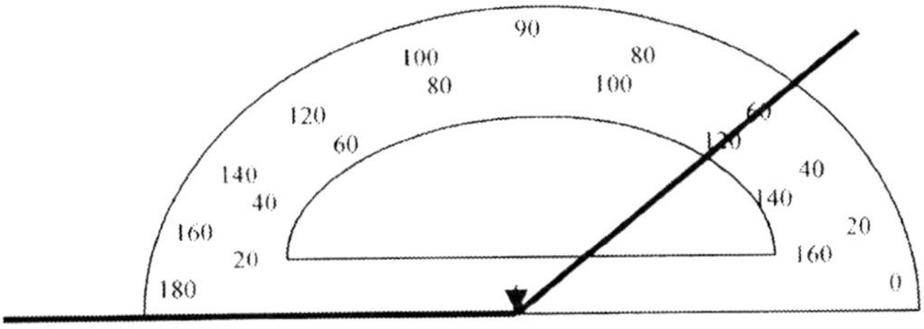

Reiterate that the acute angles (less than a square corner) are going to be less than 90 degrees, and the obtuse angles (greater than a square corner) are going to be greater than 90 degrees. Use critical thinking skills. Don't try and please the teacher with quick answers. What do YOU think? Draw an angle on the board or overhead. Is this greater than a square corner? Yes? So the protractor is going to read somewhere between 90 and 180. What do you guess it is? You think 130 degrees? Lets find out. You were very close. It is actually 138. Not bad. (Involving the students in this manner cannot be stressed enough. Do this for several obtuse, acute, and even square angles).

Areas and Perimeters

"Let's talk about a checkerboard. Counting the squares finds that there are 64. Or, 8 rows of 8 squares make 64 squares. $8 \times 8 = 64$. Lets call the lines on the squares some name, any name (get some suggestions from the class). How about "gorks?" So, 1 square is 1 square gork. That is, it is 1gork by 1 gork, or a square gork. In this shape, how many gorks are there around the outside edge? (It is suggested here that you have precut clear and colored acetate to overlay various parts of the checkerboard – in this case, 4 squares together in the shape of a square). How many gorks are there around the edge? Right! There are 8 gorks. We call that the perimeter. (Now put on an overlay of 4 squares in a row forming a rectangle). How many gorks are around the edge now? Yes, there are 10. (See if anyone discovers that with a like number of squares, there can be a different perimeter depending on the shape)."

Tell the class that knowing about perimeters puts them on a level equal to high school kids. Be liberal with compliments when they have paid attention. Have several checkerboards and divide the class into groups around each checkerboard. Their task is to make their gork rulers out of strips of tag board using one of the squares as the length of a gork. Once the rulers are made, their assignment, should they choose to accept it—just kidding—is to measure the perimeters of things around the room, such as desks, windowpanes, tables, books, etc. They are to draw the shapes and respective perimeters on one sheet of paper for the group. After 15 minutes, the class should get back into their groups and share their designs and perimeters. The homework assignment that night could be to find four things at home and measure their perimeters with their gork rulers.

The next math period should review perimeters and explore area more deeply. Still using different colored overlays of various sizes, cover one square on the checkerboard. "What is the perimeter? Right, it's 4 gorks. How many square gorks—that is, 1 gork high and 1 gork wide—do you see? One? You got it."

Next, put an overlay over a rectangle shape of 2 by 4 squares. "How many squares do you see now? Right. You counted correctly. There are 2 squares high and 4 wide to make 8 squares in all. How about this? (Put an overlay over 16 squares—4 high and 4 wide). Yes, there are 16 squares. Is there a way we can tell how many squares there are without counting each one? (The students should discover that taking the height by the width tells how many squares there are).

Proceed to lead the class in discussions about "square" numbers by asking if they have ever heard of one. The students should find that some numbers could be put in the shape of a square, such as 1, 4, 9, 16, 25, 36, *ad infinitum*. Will they discover that the numbers between each of these have a pattern to them? Perhaps with your guidance.

Anyway, back to finding the areas of figures in plane geometry. Again, divide the class into groups, each equipped with their trusty gork rulers. See if they can find objects that they can determine roughly how many gork squares will fit into them. That is how we talk about the area—how many squares will fit inside a perimeter.

Transitioning the concepts learned in gork units, and how they are used in determining perimeters and areas, easily falls into place when relating to centimeters, square centimeters, meters, square meters, inches, square inches, feet, miles, or whatever unit is desired.

The introduction to geometry via work with points, lines, angles, areas and perimeters serves as a springboard for subsequent work with finding the area of a circle (introducing pi), triangles, and other geometrical challenges. There is fertile ground for tactile and thinking activities.

STORY PROBLEMS

A sure-fire, boiler-plated, government inspected, grade A, blue ribbon, top drawer, Good Housekeeping approved, every-time-a-bull's-eye way to get kids interested in story problems is to cultivate their involvement. Kids of elementary age and into middle school love to imagine and pretend. Capitalizing on that is the basis for developing a surprising embrace of story problems. A corollary to the preceding assertion is that stories involving money will often pique the interest of the most recalcitrant students.

Pick any three kids in the class and lay out a scenario such that they are walking home and they see a brown paper sack lying in the gutter. It is kicked by (name one of the students) and it seems to have some heft to it. Embellishment of the story is purely optional. Finding a balance of time and the number of problems to accomplish should be weighed. The students and the class are enthralled as you say that Suzy carefully opens the sack and finds a rather significant wad of dollar bills of various denominations amounting to $1258.68. Naturally, there will be a morality lesson here, too, as the story continues with the kids taking the money to the police station, of course. So, when no one has claimed the money, how much does each person get when they share it equally? This could be a pre-cursor to teaching long division. Divide the class into small groups and see what they come up with. It teaches teamwork, facility with money, and usefulness of division.

Giving a student an opportunity to imagine going to a store of their choice with some money to spend is fertile ground for a myriad of math problems. It works well with even the most marked attention deficit child. The rest of the class will listen and want to know what their classmate would buy. Say the student was given money for a birthday from a distant, generous uncle. What would he or she like to buy? Keep track of the choices and how much they cost (estimate). Write the prices on the board. Will he or she have enough money? How much will it cost in all? How much change should he or she expect? How much more does one item cost than another? The possibilities are quite extensive.

Key words should be taught as a guide for solving problems, as discussed earlier in the chapter. "How much in all," or "what is the total?" of course, refers to addition and/or multiplication. "What's the difference?" involves subtraction as does "how much more," or "how much farther?" Story problems using "each," may count on dividing something into groups for the answer. Students who find math difficult need little hints like these to help them along in their thinking skills.

Here is an example of the "each" word referred to above that will probably deal with division:

"You go into a supermarket on a very hot day to buy a soda. You only want one pop. The sign says that a 6-pack of cola costs $1.80. You only have 35 cents. How much does *each* one cost in the 6-pack? Do you have enough money to buy one?" Naturally, you do not have to divide to get the answer. The students could work on various solutions such as, "OK, 6 times something equals $1.80. Let's try some numbers out and see what's up." They might start with .50 and find that is too big. At any rate, after several problems in which discoveries are made of how grouping and division works, it might be found that dividing $1.80 by 6 means that each bottle costs .30 each, and yes you do have enough money to buy one.

Knowledge of key words such as these are a help when special education students and general education students, take standardized, periodic tests that our legislators seem to think are a way to solve education's ills. It doesn't take a rocket scientist to figure out that school will become an exercise in teaching for the next test. Would that the legislators concentrate on laws that help the disenfranchised in society, such as matters that deal with health insurance, minimum wage, retirement plans, and the like. Then, perhaps parents would have more time for their children instead of having to carry two jobs to get by because a company won't make a position full-time because it would mean having to pay benefits. It is not a panacea for schools' problems, but it's a start.

A great way to exercise story problem thinking is to present a problem to the class. Making up one's own stories are the best. If Martha had gone to California last summer, making up stories about distances she had gone would be interesting for the class. Here is an example: Martha went to Los Angeles last summer. That is 3149 miles away. Blake went to Cheyenne, which is 813 miles away. How much farther did Martha travel one way than Blake?"

When presenting problems, it is fun to give points as solutions are worked on, either individually or in teams. A practice that has evolved is that if someone thinks they have the answer, they don't shout it out but raise their hand. You as the teacher check it. If it is correct, you award the points depending on the degree of difficulty. Invariably, the student who is first will ask if they can go around the room checking others when they raise their hand. It really works. Not everyone gets them right all the time. It's like life—some people are better than others at some things.

AN INTRODUCTION TO ALGEBRA

Algebra is a discipline developed in ancient Arabia in which symbols are used to take the place of unknown quantities. Algebra is derived from an Arabic word meaning the reunion of broken parts. In real time it is a useful tool that special education students have a hard time mastering, just like regular students have a hard time mastering and using it in real life if they are not prepared to grapple with it. All we are trying to do here is for the middle school student to be exposed to the basics and have an understanding of how it is used.

Instruction of the commutative, associative, and distributive properties is the place to start. In the commutative principle, it is simply a rule by which changes can be made in an equation towards isolating the unknown, which is usually represented by a symbol, such as X. The commutative property states that you can add or multiply numbers in any order and the sum or product are the same. Addition: $3 + 7 = 7 + 3$. Multiplication: $5 \times 8 = 8 \times 5$. An exercise for applying this property would be to give a set of numbers to add, such as $7 + 8 + 3$. For the challenged learner, it perhaps would be easier to think $7 + 3$ is $10 + 8$ is 18. The lesson, of course, is that you can change around the order to take the easier route. In multiplication, re-write $2 \times 8 \times 3$ to $2 \times 3 \times 8 = 48$ (Leiva & Brown, p. 26).

In the associative property, when you add or multiply three or more numbers, you can group the numbers without affecting the result. For example, $(5 + 9) + 11 = 5 + (9 + 11)$. So, if it's easier to think of $9 + 11$ is 20 plus 5 is 25, go with it. Remember, in solving equations in mathematics, do the parentheses part of a mathematical sentence, first. Here follows an example of the associative property in multiplication. By the way, since X is used so much as an unknown quantity in algebra, a mid-level dot [·] is used to indicate multiply. So, $(1/2 \cdot 5)6$ are easier to process as $1/2(5 \cdot 6)$, which equals 15. (Leiva & Brown, p. 26)

The distributive property may be used to write equivalent expressions, or mathematical sentences that mean the same thing. Note: when a number is right next to a parentheses or a symbol, it means to multiply it, such that 2x is the same as 2 times x, or 2(4+2) is the same as 2 times 6. Back to the distributive property: $5(22 + 4) = 5 \cdot 22 + 5 \cdot 4$. (Leiva & Brown, p.35) An exercise in re-writing one side of the equation to the other, applying the distributive property, is a do-able and fun exercise for the algebra novices

Use multiplication or division to solve an equation (Larson, p. 71). Whatever you do to one side, do to the other. How about this one: 5 X = 20. Divide both sides by 5 which is:

$$\frac{5\,x}{5} = \frac{20}{5}$$

$$x = 4$$

Here's one:

$$12 = {}^{n}/4$$

Multiply both sides by 4:

$$4 \times 12 = 4 \times {}^{n}/4$$

The right side of this equation is simply "n" because you cancel the 4s and it looks like this:

$$\frac{4}{1} \times \frac{n}{4} = \frac{n}{1} = n$$

$$48 = n$$

Having tasted algebraic equations—an equation, so called because the two sides always equal each other—let's try a whole plate. Go through some equations like the following, encouraging them to think as you ask questions.

$$2x - 2 = 0$$

In order to solve this, you have to isolate x. Whatever you do to one side of the equation, you must do to the other. To get rid of the -2, add 2 to both sides. Now you have

$$2x - 2 + 2 = 0 + 2$$

Now, simplify by combining the numerals. -2 plus + 2 is 0, or nothing, so wipe it out. 0 + 2 is 2 so simplify by getting rid of the 0. Now you have

$$2x = 2$$

What can we do to whittle the equation down even further? It's fairly clear that x = 1, because 2 times one equals 2. For the sake of showing how it's done, let's make it more basic. How about if we divided both sides by 2? The easy way to show divide is to make a line and put what you are dividing by underneath.

$$\frac{2x}{2} = \frac{2}{2}$$

/ \

2 into 2 is 1, so you have 1x = 1. Anytime you have a 1 by a symbol, just put the symbol. Thus:

2 into 2 is 1

$$x = 1$$

Ta da!

Try this one:

$$3x - 6 = x + 2$$

Simplify by getting rid of the –6.
Do so by adding 6 to both sides.

$$3x + 6 - 6 = x + 2 + 6$$

You can clean this up by thinking that 6 – 6 is nothing so you get rid of the 6's on the left side. 2 and 6 is combined to 8 on the right side. You have simplified the equation to

$$3x = x + 8$$

To simplify further, subtract an x from both sides.

$$3x - x = x - x + 8$$

This results in

$$2x = 8$$

Divide both sides by 2 and you will have the clear answer.

$$\frac{2x}{2} = \frac{8}{2}$$

$$x = 4$$

How about that!

Sadly, a lot of schools and teachers give up on special education students, and general education students, for that matter. There are elements of algebra to which all middle school students should be exposed. A little energy and excitement about it will sow the seed of potential fruition. A little watering with self-discipline could reap a bountiful harvest of knowledge and self-respect. These are the yields, that when stored in the loft, may be called upon in high school's times of need.

MATH FOOTBALL

As a culminating activity for a week's worth of hard work in math, the last half of Friday's class period is devoted to Math Football. There will be no homework assignment for the week-end except to go outside, have fun, get dirty, and enjoy the days off. After going over a lesson in the first part of the period, the students anticipate "the game" with a good deal of enthusiasm. Teams are decided by various methods that an effective teacher has deftly refined. Team captains are appointed, usually from a pool of students that earned an "A" on their assignment. They are responsible for naming and moving around the football positions. A nerf football is used. There is a QB who attempts to throw a pass to one of two receivers that go out for a pass. It may require moving desks, somewhat. At the front of the room is the team with the ball. The QB stands in the middle of the line of scrimmage, which is across the front of the room, with two receivers on the extreme left and right of the line, ready to amble down the two outside aisles. The teacher shows the QB a multiplication flash card. If the QB gets it right, he or she may proceed. If the QB gets it wrong, it's a *fumble* and the other team takes over on offense. So, assuming the QB gets it right, he or she holds the nerf football and says, "Down, set, hike!" The two receivers head down to the other end of the room. The defensive team is allowed one defensive back who stands three quarters of the way toward the back of the room in the middle, facing the front. The rest of the defensive team has to stand along the wall or windows to one side, out of play. The quarterback attempts to throw the football to one of the receivers in the right or left corner while the lone defensive back tries to intercept or knock the ball down by guessing which way the QB is going to throw. If they complete a pass, it is a touchdown, or six points. An extra point can then be attempted, which is tossing the football to a wastepaper basket half way across the room. If the football goes in, it's two points. If it only touches the wastebasket it's just one point. If they miss it altogether, it's no points. The team scoring the touchdown has to add the score correctly under the team name on the board. The other team takes over and the process repeats. Variations may develop by allowing the two receivers to surreptitiously switch or move along a line at the back of the room. The defensive back has to stay in front of the end zone and cannot turn around to see where the receivers are. It is not wild. It actually lends itself well to a classroom with the desks moved a little bit to make for lanes and an end zone. If all in the class come to know all the multiplication flash cards fairly well as the year progresses, you could have the QB and the defensive back vie for who gets the flash card answered first. If it's the defensive back that wins, it's a fumble. If the QB is first, then they proceed as described above. The game is a powerful motivational tool. If a student did not complete his or her assignment, he or she will be sitting on the sidelines while the others are playing. Perhaps that will happen once. The next time they will have the homework assignment done.

Chapter 6
Making Social Studies Fun

Two teachers of social studies were overheard to say that they did not like using a textbook in class because textbooks are boring. How unfortunate. They are depriving a lot of students from learning a lot of information. The school system that purchased textbooks for their social studies curriculum would take a dim view of such a philosophy. However, it seems typical of social studies classes in schools today. There is a lot of drawing and coloring of quasi-historical scenes, village making, pyramid building, cartouche creating, artifact artwork, and other model making without the discipline of gathering information.

Variety is what makes scholastic pursuit interesting in middle school. While the above activities are fun and meaningful, too much of it can be deadly. And, there may not be a lot of knowledge gained. Stories abound in which there is a dearth of basic knowledge of United States' history exhibited by average citizens. Here is an article entitled "Don't Know Much About History," by Vicki Hughes, reprinted with permission:

> I usually let David Letterman put me to sleep, but David was a re-run the other night, so I let Jay Leno have the honors. He did his job admirably, and I was asleep before his monologue was over.
>
> It was the next morning that the trouble began. You see, I also tape the show to watch while I read my morning newspaper. In those early morning hours, I was appalled to watch something called "JayWalking" where Jay goes out on the street to ask common citizens (albeit California) questions.

This time, he was asking about famous war battles, because the movie Pearl Harbor was about to be released. He started with the obvious question, "Have you heard of Pearl Harbor?" His first victim had not only heard of the movie but ventured to guess that Pearl Harbor occurred in 1967 when the Chinese people invaded America.

I'd like to say she was the exception, but the next person informed us that Pearl Harbor was "a long time ago" and it was bombed (so far, so good) by ...the Hawaiians! She went on to tell us that the Hawaiians won.

The next person to be interviewed was a guy who accurately knew that Pearl Harbor was the start of World War II. (Baby Boomers—let's not quibble on international relations—you couldn't expect him to know that the war was being fought for two years prior to Pearl Harbor). He went on to tell us that Pearl Harbor occurred on Dec. 19, 1924.

Flash back to the second girl to be interviewed—you remember, the one who thought the Hawaiians bombed Pearl Harbor. She was asked when Pearl Harbor occurred. She guessed...1960, 1965, 1970, then decided that since she was born in 1970, it must have been in 1969. Lincoln turns in his grave.

It gets worse (if that's possible!). Leno asked the next person about the Civil War. She confidently answered that the Civil War was fought between the United States and Germany and that the "Getty People" fought at the Battle of Gettysburg.

Next came a teacher—finally, some correct answers, right? Sorry. She informed us that the Confederates warned the Northerners that the British were coming. There's more, but I just can't go on. I must stop to rant.

We cannot allow entire generations to grow into adulthood with such a vague and downright erroneous version of our country's history. Hoping for a concept of international history appears to be fruitless. I know these people were chosen for the "comedy" of their answers. I was just about to cease my

> ranting. I even put these words aside for several days. Then came a Friday night "College Edition of 'Who Wants to be a Millionaire.'" The first contestant was a lovely young woman who was a freshman at Emory University—not exactly a second-class institute of higher learning. However, she failed to know that the United States had only 48 states at the beginning of World War I. What's going on?
>
> The ranting continues. What are we teaching the youth of America? Are we so focused on technology that we are neglecting the basics? Educators, what is the status of our education system today? Have we left reading, writing, arithmetic and history behind as unimportant? These are serious questions, and they deserve serious answers. I, for one, would like to know.

The heinous act at the World Trade Center is less real than some middle school students' pursuit of *Zelda* or playing *Star Wars* on video games. Will September 11, 2001 be a date "which will live in infamy" and remembered like December 7, 1941? We must emphasize our nation's foundation and crucible events. Without a collective identity of history, the lives of young people will become trivialized into an acquisitive pursuit of material gain and instant gratification.

Social Studies GeoParty

One way to help social studies students become familiar with the social studies textbook, atlas, and the world around them is to play *Social Studies GeoParty*. This is based somewhat on the game show, *Jeopardy*, only by the grid of categories and increasing degrees of value for answering questions. In this game there are only four categories and they're always the same. They are: "Using a Textbook," "Using an Atlas," "General Social Studies," and "General Knowledge."

One of the attributes of this game is the ease with which it can be set up and played. You simply write the four headings on the chalkboard. Underneath the headings you stick post-its with the values of the questions, starting with 10 across the first row, 20 on the second, then 30, 40, and 50 along the bottom row. Each heading will have a column of post-its below it numbering 10 to 50. The teacher will have all the questions on a sheet of paper. When a student, or team of students, picks a category and an amount, the teacher will read the question from the sheet, which has been set up to look like the board, but without the little post-its. So, team A may say, "Using a Textbook for 30." The teacher reads the 3rd question down from the textbook column, which might be something like, "When did Alexander the Great Live?" If the students have listened to instruction about the textbook whereby an index is a sure-fire way to start searching for information, they may arrive at an answer. If correct, you take off the post-it with the "30" on it and give it to the players that got it right. At the end of the game, the teams will have accumulated points based on the value of the post-it notes.

It works better to go from team to team without the competition of someone buzzing in the quickest. You give each team about a minute, or so, and if unsuccessful, the next team in rotation picks a category and amount. Using yellow post-its with numbers written on them, the chalkboard would look like this:

USING A TEXTBOOK	USING AN ATLAS	GENERAL SOC. STUDIES	GENERAL KNOWLEDGE
10	10	10	10
20	20	20	20
30	30	30	30
40	40	40	40
50	50	50	50

During the game, the teacher will hold a sheet with all the questions such as the following:

Using a Textbook	Using an Atlas	Gen. Social Studies	Gen. Knowledge
On p. 413, what was the dominant religion of Portugal in 1618?	What is farther away from us, Des Moines or Waterloo?	Who is the current governor or our state?	Who won the last Super Bowl?
Name two products of Switzerland.	What Great Lake is the farthest west?	Name a state in the Confederacy during our Civil War.	Name 4 planets of our solar system.
On p. 219, what percentage of Athens' population were slaves?	In what U.S. state does the Snake River rise or start in?	Put in order of their occurrence: WW I, Civil War, Viet Nam War, and WW II.	Who starred in the movie *Jumanji*?
When did Napoleon Bonaparte live?	What city is at 30 degrees N, and 90 degrees W?	What causes the seasons?	What is 100 ×100?
On pp. 542 & 543, if it's 12:00 noon in London, what time is it in Chicago?	Which is the most mountainous, Hungary, Belgium, or Italy?	What causes the ocean tides?	What fruit do these mixed-up letters spell?: TRAPICO

Religions of the World

As cited throughout this book, variety cannot be emphasized enough. In fact, it is the mantra for teachers who want to have control while guiding the students in meaningful learning. One day, read from a textbook, together, following the guidelines described in other parts of this book. On another day, do a map exercise—coloring is always popular. Intersperse the curriculum with research projects that involve individual efforts or small-group work. A topic that most world history textbooks address is religion. This topic lends itself well to a customized unit based on research of assigned countries and their most prevalent religions or state religions. For example, Israel is associated with Judaism. India, Hinduism. Thailand, Buddhism. Saudi Arabia, Islam. Italy, Christianity. Japan, the way of Shinto. Naturally, one should emphasize that not all peoples of the assigned countries are necessarily believers of the faith associated with it. This could generate discussions about the differences between state religions and countries that embrace freedom of religion. There are ample statistics on the percentages of religious practitioners in each country. There are several avenues to take in consideration of world religions. Pique interest by discussing what major events in human history were the results of religious beliefs? What conflicts today center around religion? Some topics are best considered at the end of the unit, such as: How are the religions similar? How are they different?

Assigning the groups should take into consideration individual characteristics and learning styles of the students. Depending on the size of the class the groups could be from two to four people. Match people who are more verbal with those whose strong points are visually adept at reading. Most teachers will know the nuances of personalities that would make a good team. When the unit is introduced, a contract sheet is helpful. It should list what is expected, a place to write who they are working with, and a place to write the names of their country and religion. The clearer the expectations, the better the results. Each responsibility should be listed numerically. Here is an example of a religion unit contract:

RELIGION AND COUNTRY UNIT

My name is ______________. Others in my group are ______________ ______________. We are doing a report on the country of ______________ and the religion of ______________. Other members of the group and I will do the following to successfully complete the religion unit:

1. Make a white construction paper cutout in the shape of the assigned country. Across it write the name of the country in big, colorful letters. Put a star where the capital city is and write its name by it. Draw and color a facsimile of that country's flag on it. Lastly, a colored construction paper backing on it. When an oral report is finished, your efforts will hang from a mobile with all the other countries in the classroom. The country will be about the size of a sheet of construction paper.

2. Do research from various sources, such as textbooks, encyclopedias, the Internet, and atlases to gather at least 7 facts about the assigned country. Practice presenting the facts for an oral report to the class.

3. Likewise, do research from various sources to gather 7 facts about the assigned religion. Practice presenting the facts for an oral report to the class.

4. Make a symbol of the assigned religion on a sheet of construction paper with a different colored backing, which also will hang on the mobile.

Signature: ______________

This has all the elements—tracing, cutting, coloring, maps, and specific research - that make it a fun couple of weeks in social studies. When making the design of the country on construction paper, it works best to trace a country on a transparency from an atlas. Put the transparency on the overhead and project it on the target paper taped to the wall. Trace the outline and cut out same. Voila! There is your country's shape writ large. For a culminating activity that lasts the rest of the year is to put their countries and religious symbols in a mobile and hang it in the room.

As a precursor to the religion unit, a very evocative activity that demonstrates the cultural relativism of belief systems is the following: Set it up by saying that some anthropologists observed a most curious ritual by an unnamed culture. Divide the class into groups of 3 or 4 and hand each of the groups the following report:

The observed society has various activities and institutions of different levels of importance. One ritual, however, seems to be of particular value because it is practiced daily by all the members of a kinship group, usually on arising in the morning and just before entering into respective sleeping arrangements at night. The location of these rituals can best be described as a shrine. Sometimes there is more than one shrine in a family unit habitation, but the rituals are conducted privately, not in groups.

Behind a closed entryway individuals engage in some preliminary activities in readiness for worship. At the moment of approach to the shrine's focal point, the worshipers pay homage by becoming very animated, such as smiling, frowning, showing ones tongue, turning the head while maintaining eye contact, and often drawing ones face in close, widening the eyes, perhaps as a display of sincerity and truthfulness. This object of attention is a shallow, rectangular box on a wall at eye level. Sometimes the box's door is swung open to reveal potions and balms that are taken internally or applied externally, sometimes with great care.

Upon exiting the shrine, participants in the rites seem to have a satisfied, although less animated countenance. That is, they are not showing their tongue or teeth, or making faces. They may not revisit the place of worship until later in the evening. Whether the worshipers of this culture visit other shrines away from the domiciles is unknown. The observations only involved the living places of the kinship units and not the hunting, gathering, or other cultural functions of the group.

Ask the students to read the report silently while you read it aloud, illuminating some parts, if necessary. In their groups, ask the students to discuss and answer some questions.

1. What can you say about the people of this society?

2. Why do the people worship in the shrine?

3. Is the god they worship kind? Is their god mean?

4. What is the purpose of making faces in the ritual?

5. Is this society advanced or backward in their technology?

After the groups have done their work and shared some of their findings, tell the class that the culture under study is actually us. The activities, which seem like religious rituals, are really what we look like in front of a mirror or medicine cabinet in a bathroom. Use this opportunity to discuss how different cultures have different values and customs. If what we find in other cultures seems silly, just remember how we may look to others.

Viewing Video Tapes

Students of this day and age tend to grow weary of seeing videos. Why? Certainly not, because this author has shown a lot of videos. No, it seems to be a function of television and video game overload. They get exposed to so much visual media out of school. They don't want to have to sit through it in school, if it's done too much. There are so many ways to justify showing some of the great movies of historical significance. Or, of course, there are vast amounts of educational videos available. And, videotapes are so easy to use. Just pop one in a VCR, and *voila!* You're all set. For awhile you're not on stage.

As you remove tongue from cheek, you realize that this book is not a recommendation for the use of videos. No, but sometimes they are edifying and attention-grabbing. Do not overuse. When you do show a videotape, here's a technique to make it a pleasant experience. When the video is over, ask the students to think of a question for the class about what they just saw. If they have a question that is answered by someone, they get a point and the answerer gets a point. After a couple of videos have been reviewed in this manner, you will find that the students are taking notes, voluntarily, of what they are seeing. I think many social studies teachers take the joy of watching a video by insisting that the students take notes. In this way, the teachers are justifying showing a video by saying to the students that the video is important. It is so important that you should take notes on it. Unfortunately, the students miss a lot when they concentrate on trying to take notes on everything. When it's voluntary, it's more meaningful.

Reading the Textbook

As suggested earlier, textbooks offer a vast amount of information on any subject. If the subject happens to be social studies, in all likelihood textbooks for your classroom have been purchased by the local school district that reflect its curriculum goals for your grade level in social studies. If you do not avail yourself to that resource, you are essentially refuting a process that selected that textbook, as well as denying your students exposure to a lot of valuable information.

Variety is the operable word when it comes to teaching social studies in special education, or for difficult general education classes, too. You can't always entertain your students with hands-on materials, nor would I recommend reading all the time. Don't expect a special education class to read selections by themselves. It is unrealistic to think that you could sit back at a desk while your class reads and absorbs selections from a textbook. It won't work. That's why they're in special education, oftentimes with reading problems. Make your lesson plans practical with small objectives in mind. Everyday can be a learning experience just by being in your classroom. It's better than a child sitting in a cave with no stimulation. Don't become bogged down in edu-canese and the latest buzz word, such as "benchmark." Sometimes you just read information, absorb it, and discuss it. Of course, your lesson plans should specify how much material to cover. That's what this segment is about.

Pass out the textbooks and find the selection for the day's lesson. Introduce the topic by summarizing, briefly, what the selection is about. Ask pertinent questions to generate some interest. Point out some difficult words. Begin reading aloud. Stop somewhere and see if anybody knows what the next word is. If so, raising a hand to say the word earns a point. Soon, the students will be following along with intense interest. If three or four students raise their hands simultaneously, tell them to say the word together on the count of three. Give each a point, that is, tell the scorekeeper to mark down a point to each. The students will want to read aloud, too. By all means let them, but help them pronounce words they have difficulty with. They may stop on occasion, too, and call on someone who knows what the next word is, thus earning a point. The readers get a point for reading. This method accommodates reading materials that may be several years ahead of the students.

To cover a lot of information, tell the class you are going to read as fast as you can, that you are going to give them your best shot. You doubt that they can follow along and keep up, but they can try. They invariably take the challenge. Of course they can keep up. Scanning along with the eyes can go ever so much faster than you can say the words. The act of looking at words while you read them is sure to increase the students' sight-word vocabulary. You won't find this fact in any other reading publication, but now you know. Most professional articles about reading generally follow a basic pattern: Yes, phonics are important, but the whole-language approach, i.e., variety of instruction, is the most effective. The general tone of these articles seem aimed at impressing colleagues with vocabulary and sacrificing clear writing for statistical obfuscation and self-promotion. Why use terms such as, "sounding-out words" and "reading practice" when "phonemic awareness" and "metacognitive activities" sounds so much more impressive?

Reading improvement basically comes from direct instruction about phonics, reading aloud, and looking at words while others read. Just practicing bringing the voice down conclusively for the period at the end of a sentence helps the struggling reader a great deal. I've noticed most special education kids who are behind in reading do not pay any attention to a period. They just read word after word after word. There is no feeling for the rhythm and sentence structure of prose. Therefore, there is less comprehension. Monitoring this and other facets of the reading process, such as helping the student sound out words with encouragement and positive comments, provides growth in reading skills. There is not a significant difference with this methodology employed in groups or individuals. What's the big secret about learning to read? Practice. Practice. Practice.

Teaching Outline Form

There are so many ways to teach the different units that are prescribed by the school systems. Again, the key is variety. Intersperse creative and imaginative lessons throughout the unit. One day fill in a map with countries and color it. The next day, read pages in a textbook and discuss. The next day work on an assigned, in-depth, individualized, research topic (which will take several days throughout the unit). The next day, focus on a lesson about the outline form. Here's a creative way to teach the outline form and taking notes. Create a lecture on a topic to deliver to the class. Say a topic on communism in the China unit. Type it on big type and make a transparency of your outline for projecting on the screen during your lecture. Have a cover sheet which you pull down slowly to reveal point by point the essence of your lecture. Your students will have the same outline, except on their copy they have words left out here and there in the sub points below the main points. Their task is to fill in the blanks on their copies by listening and reading the outline form projected on the screen. The class is captivated by your lecture! You are sharing the outline technique, teaching how to take notes, and imparting knowledge at the same time.

General Social Studies

There are so many ways to teach the social studies curriculum. The subjects depend on the local school districts. Whatever they are, the approach should involve imaginative and creative ways to make the topics interesting. However, don't short-change the students by not using a textbook. There is so much information to be gained by reading the materials. To enrich and expand upon what you have read is to live it and make it real. Suppose you have read how early humans were wont to interpret their lives of hunting and surviving in a hostile world by making cave paintings of life around them. You read how the prehistoric tribes went to considerable trouble to make torches, paint, and brushes and journeyed far to leave part of their culture on cave walls. Go with that. Spend a period going outside to gather colored rocks to pulverize into a paint base. Or, gather sticks and weeds and fashion into paintbrushes. If you take a stick and pound one end into fibers, it makes a handy paintbrush, perhaps just like our ancestors actually used eons ago. (I have found that experiencing the attempt to crush rocks or gather berries for making paint is a lesson well learned. However, when actually painting "caves," tempura paint and paintbrushes work well. Charcoal and sticks pulverized on one end work well, too).

Now for a cave to paint. In our building there is a huge auditorium with a balcony and hallways leading from it. It is generally dark and unused during the day. In one of the hallways I taped a long piece of brown paper on a wall. For torches, use bright yellow goldenrod paper rolled up and taped to the lighted end of a flashlight. There. You have torches that look like the real thing in the dark. Tell the class that we have a dangerous journey in the dark past cliffs (balcony) in a huge cave. Everyone makes their way to the (brown paper) cave wall armed with torches, brushes, and paint. It is an atavistic mission that puts you in the mindset of the ancients leaving their mark on cave walls. It's so real! Regardless of the kind of building you're in, there must be some dark places where this can be done.

Put your minds in this creative mode to teach lessons. Read about cultural ways in China? Get some very inexpensive chopsticks (40 for .75¢) and teach them to eat dry Chinese noodles with chopsticks. A unit on encroachment of white settlers into Native Americans' land? Paint a big rock gold. Divide the class into settlers and Native Americans. Let the Native Americans go outside and hide the gold, after which they may go about the school grounds hunting and gathering coupons (which you have hidden) that can be redeemed for a reward, such as food. In the meantime, tell the settlers they have to find the gold in order to have rewards. Turn the settlers loose and watch to what extent they will go to find the gold as they encroach on the Native Americans' activities. There is absolutely no limit on well-planned, safe, enlightening social studies activities, but they must be preceded by preparation, rules, and follow-up discussions on what the students gained from the activity.

Chapter 7
Science is...Experiments!

This chapter, like other subjects in this book, is not meant to be a compendium of methods for teaching science. It is geared toward offering some ideas to make your classroom a place where kids want to be. If that is accomplished, classroom management is much easier to maintain. That is the philosophy of this whole book: overwhelm your students with energy and enthusiasm, and learning is sure to follow.

Science textbooks try to make their books interesting, as though they were competing with video games and television. Therefore, they tend to have a lot of pictures, different colors, cartoons, and randomly placed *froufrou* around the pages. This practice is not limited to just science textbooks. Most textbooks in our schools are adopting this "look." It can be distracting, but it's a sign of the frenetic times we live in. Time is not money—it is competition for brief attention spans. Textbooks are geared to the young students so they will not be daunted by a page of just text, which might be considered boring—the bane of the adolescent mind.

The school system in which this author toils has adopted *Science Plus* as its science curriculum textbook. Holt, Rinehart, and Winston will say it's not just a textbook, but also a system for teaching science. They are right. There have produced a good deal of materials that enhances the units of study. The textbook has a lot of illustrations and pictures that invite further inquiry. It is infused throughout with evocative questions that are just begging for a student generated hypothesis. There are workbooks for each unit, video explorations, CD's, and interactive computer programs. It is quite user-friendly. The authors and developers did not scrimp on the variety of presentations of science curriculum. I am a firm believer in good textbooks, which is the reason I use them and have developed methods for making the reading of them included in the variety pack of classroom work.

It is to be hoped that your school system is solvent enough to purchase a good textbook for your science education. If not, you can still teach engaging science without the concomitant and ancillary materials now found with newly purchased educational materials these days. The key to teaching successful science to reluctant learners or students with disabilities is to have a lot of experiments. They should be easy to set up and inexpensive. True, the textbook *Science Plus* has a lot of experiments described in its book. They also have a form that is just excellent for conducting an experiment:

Hypothesis
Experiment
Results
Conclusion

One of the goals in science is to have a working knowledge of what the scientific method is. After doing a few experiments that are set up properly, the students will know what the scientific method is—by experience—not by trying to memorize the steps in the scientific method. The students will discover that any experiment should be able to be repeated and arrive at the same results. Also, they will find that they can keep everything the same (control group) in one experiment and simultaneously do another in which only one thing is changed (a variable), and see if they produce different results. Quick example: Get a couple of empty, large fruit drink bottles. In both, just the same, put in some dirt, some seeds—such as grass, cucumber, or beans—and water. In one of the jars, call it the experimental one, add fertilizer. In the other jar, call it the control jar, do not add fertilizer. Make observations over the next 10 days. It's a good visualization of a controlled experiment.

You can invent your own experiments that are easy to set up and result in a flash of insight. These are the best kind of experiments for persons who may have short attention spans. They should have the opportunity for helping to set up experiments, too. I have found that students love to have things to do with their hands, especially things that are helping the overall conduct of the classroom. This may sound contrary to notions about the reluctant student, but sometimes students who have difficulties haven't been given the opportunity to do things that are positive and helpful. It could be things like cleaning off the overhead projector, straightening books in a bookshelf, passing out papers, or getting materials ready for an experiment. Anyway, students in science are an excellent resource for assistance in a variety of tasks.

Here's an experiment about gravity. Ask the class what would happen if you simultaneously dropped a bowling ball and a marble from a high place. What would hit the ground first? Most people, not just kids, will say the bowling ball because it is heavier. Of course Galileo proved that gravity acts the same on mass regardless of its weight by dropping metal balls of different weight from the leaning tower of Pisa. They all hit the ground at the same time. In a moment of mischievous fun, Scott Carpenter dropped a hammer and a feather at the same time on the moon where there is no atmosphere to divert the feather's drop, and they hit bottom at exactly the same time. I happen to teach in a four-story building. The anticipation of seeing a bowling ball and a marble dropped from a 4th floor window onto the ground generates a lot of interest. Safety precautions are followed, such as making the class stand back on the sidewalk as the marble and the bowling ball thud into the soft ground. Prior to the actual experiment, use your experiment form. Start with a question that the student would like to know, like, "Will a heavy object fall faster than a lighter object?" Turn the question into the form of an hypothesis, such as, "A bowling ball will drop from a height of 20 meters faster than a marble." Then, draw a model of what will take place, making it very simple, such as a building, window, bowling ball, and marble, labeling all. The next section will be for what the students observed. Draw a schematic of the bowling ball and marble dropping and hitting the ground at the same time. Write a short synopsis of the results, in this case, no difference was observed between the rates of the marble's and the bowling ball's descent. At the bottom is a place for a conclusion: Gravity acts on objects the same way regardless of their weight.

Here's one. Hypothesis: Water will bend light. Experiment: In an opaque dish about the size of a whipped cream container, tape a coin, such as a quarter, in the middle of the bottom. Walk backward until you can no longer see the coin taped to the bottom. Pour water into the dish. You will see the coin reappear! (Morrison, p.27). This can be set up using the form above and drawing a picture of what you are going to do. Then drawing the results. It doesn't have to be a work of art – just a schematic of what's happening. Then write a conclusion. What science!

Perhaps you are talking about air pressure. Is it very strong? Strong? See if you can demonstrate the force of air pressure using a glass of water and fill it half way up. Put a piece of paper on top of it and turn the glass over. What happens? Can you explain it? (The water will stay in the glass because of air pressure in the atmosphere pushing on the paper as it wants to fill the vacuum created in that space above the water in the glass). You will want to use those rectangular plastic tubs at each station.

Not all experiments have to use the experiment form described above. *Science Plus* describes a data sheet on which there are three columns. On the left you have a heading called "Activity". The middle is headed "Observations". The column on the right third of the page is headed "Inferences". Take an experiment called "Lights Out #1." Put a candle standing straight up from an aluminum pie plate. Place a beaker over a lighted candle. What happens. On the data sheet, the students would write "Lights Out #1" in the activity column. They would record that the candle went out in the observation column. In the inference column they would make an educated guess as to why the candle would no longer burn (Morrison, p. 28).

On the data sheet directly above, and using the same candle, another experiment called "Lights Out #2," could be recorded. Prepare a beaker with 30 mL of baking soda and pour in about the same amount of vinegar. Wait about 1 minute. Tip the beaker with the baking soda and vinegar solution over the candle while being careful not to pour out the solution. The candle will go out because carbon dioxide gas was formed when the baking soda and vinegar combined. Carbon dioxide is heavier than air and will "pour" out onto the flame and put it out (Morrison, p. 28). Of course you won't tell all this to the kids, but let them make observations and an inferences, which may lead to some interesting discussions.

Is it better to wear dark or light clothing in hot weather, or does it make any difference? Take two soda bottles. Paint one of them white and one of them black. Stretch a deflated balloon's mouth over the top of each bottle so they droop to the side of the bottle. Position a light bulb between the two bottles. Turn on the light and watch how the black bottle will very soon begin to inflate the balloon on its top. The balloon on the white bottle will not inflate. The dark bottle absorbs the heat and light emitted by the light bulb and the temperature rises inside, expanding the air into the balloon. No wonder that to be cool, light colored clothing is better than dark in the summer. This experiment is great for the middle school science class. It can lead off an interesting unit on light and color, or many directions you may wish to take, such as how molecules will expand in heat and contract in cold.

How about demonstrating Newton's first law of motion? You know, that's the one where either an object tends to stay in motion unless acted upon by another force, or a body tends to stay at rest unless acted upon by another force. This tendency to either keep moving or stay in place is called *inertia.* In a doorway or lab assembly, suspend about 50 cm's of button warp thread hanging straight down. It must be quite secure because you're going to be yanking down on the whole assembly. Tie a 1,000 gram weight to the bottom of the thread. Below the 1,000 gram weight, tie another thread so you have about 50 cm's of thread hanging down. Pull slowly on the bottom thread. The top thread above the weight will break. Retie the thread. Now, yank quickly on the bottom thread. The bottom thread will break as the weight stays undisturbed. Why? When pulling slowly, the weight will assist and break the upper thread. But when yanking, the 1,000 gram weight will want to stay where it is (inertia), and the lower thread will break.

There are lots of experiments such as these to make your science class interesting. Peruse various publications for ideas, or think up your own. It's up to you to make science interesting. When you make your students part of what you are doing, they will buy into it. Each student should have a science log notebook in which their data or experiment sheets should be placed, or other science activities. Students should add interesting articles that are found in newspapers or magazines related to science as the year goes along. Your enthusiasm about science is what spices up any preparation that you may do.

Chapter 8
What's It All About, LD?

American education has become bogged down in over-analyzing everything. Everybody wants to get into the act. National and state legislators are passing laws about which they know little. The "Leave No Child Behind" legislation is like Lake Wobegon where all the children are above average—it's unrealistic, even impossible. School systems have become top-heavy with superfluous administrators. The teachers in the trenches blindly follow the administrative disciple of the latest guru. Teachers have to follow along or they're out of the loop, not a team player, and insubordinate. Demands on the teachers to cure society's ills leaves less and less time for academic teaching.

There should be a national curriculum. Each grade across the country should be studying the same thing at the same time. A national committee of professors and educators under the aegis of the Department of Education should establish what is important in raising responsible citizens and turn it into a national curriculum. If a student doesn't meet each grade's minimum standard, they don't pass. Knowing this, starting at an early age, students would have an incentive to be attentive, to do homework, and attend school. No more automatic passes. They would acquire thinking skills and a knowledge base necessary to begin each year. Parents would do more to help make their children successful.

You laugh at a national curriculum? If so, you have not been a teacher. The peripatetic nature of our society means that millions of students move around each year in the middle of a school year. A child moving from Peoria to Denver should be able to fit right in without missing a beat. Teachers see how much is lost every time a student moves to a different school—even if it's just across town.

With a national curriculum, there could be a list of approved vendors of materials. There are too many salespersons selling ideas and the latest packages that are guaranteed to improve scholastic performance. Schools spend tons of money on materials that are not necessary. An enthusiastic teacher could teach reading using a Penney's catalog. There are many ways of enriching any basic textbook, but it takes preparation. Are teachers ready to do that, or do they have to have everything spelled out for them in package deals purchased by a school system at considerable cost?

On January 8, 2002, President Bush signed into law the No Child Left Behind Act of 2001. Among several things it mandated testing in grade levels to measure performance on state-created standards in reading and math followed by science standards later. If specified levels of performance by the students are not met, their school will be ineligible for Federal funding and will be subject to other forms of censure. Tests will be sorted by economically disadvantaged, racial or ethnic minority groups, disabilities, and limited English proficiency. Hello? Is anybody listening? That really does nothing for public education in America. If they really wanted to help public education, they would put the onus on the students, not the teachers. Yes, this book has already expended ink on addressing some teachers' lack of commitment to the individual student and the art of teaching. That still goes. It's up to principals and school systems to see that good teachers are hired, good teaching is being done in the classrooms, and ineffective teachers are phased out. Teachers will do their part, but students have to do their part. If Congress would change that legislation to read that if students didn't meet the requirements of each grade level, students will not be pass to the next grade. Congress should finance this by providing funds to hire teachers to absorb the grade levels that would bulge with students who didn't pass. When students realize that they aren't getting a free pass, they would do their homework, they would show up for tests, and they would wrestle with some pesky academic demands. One of the criterion for schools showing improvement in the No Child Left Behind act is that schools have to have a 95% participation in mandated tests in 3rd, 8th, and 11th

grades. Schools are already having to use various incentives to get students to come to school on the days of tests. This is absurd!

The No Child Left Behind Act sounds good. No legislator wants to be associated with leaving a child behind. It's a "feel good" type of legislation that venal legislators pass to assuage their guilt at being bought by big business. The special education laws are an example of this kind of legislation. They were meant to improve learning, but they had unintended consequences. Yes, we need a recipe for dealing with students who fall into specific mental disabilities. The boundaries of this condition are quite easy to establish and measure with IQ tests. But the legislation has gone too far when it created this arbitrary construct called "learning disabilities." It is too vague and capricious. It has undermined education in the United States more than people realize.

As cited earlier in this book, the whole learning disabled paradigm at its onset was a result of the Cold War version of "leave no child behind." Back then it meant, "leave no child behind the Russians." It also had racial overtones. If white Johnny couldn't read it was a learning disability. If black Johnny couldn't read, he must be mentally retarded. So the very concept of a learning disability had specious beginnings.

I understand that some kids have inexplicable difficulties, such as letter reversals as with the medical model called dyslexia, but those cases are very rare. You can't blame vast numbers of students in the United States that read below grade level on dyslexia. There is something else going on, but to resignedly throw up one's arms and say it's due to a learning disability is not making teachers accountable for teaching, and it is not making students accountable for learning. By the time an LD child of elementary school reaches middle school you can see how the lack of grappling with problems has become ingrained. Thinking is a learned and practiced skill. If they haven't developed it by the time they reach middle school, it is very difficult to break the mold. We are not doing them any favors by giving them a free pass. They must practice reading and applying themselves and learning to think. Furthermore, a free pass does nothing for their self-image and disallows the wonderful feeling of having accomplished something with hard work.

Yes, the learning disabled category must be phased out. No, we should not get rid of all the LD teachers. Their skills at motivation and approaching problems in innovative ways are too valuable. We still need "special" teachers (in addition to teachers in MD and BD programs) to help bring all students along in education, but we can do without all the paper work involved with an IEP. I envision special teachers who teach and help any kid in the general education venue who is having difficulties without having to go through the time consuming processes to get them the help or labeling them learning disabled. Parents don't want meaningless paperwork, they want their children to get good grades, acquire thinking skills, and to pass into the next grade when they are ready. As suggested earlier, special teachers should counsel general education teachers in the art of teaching. That is not to say that the LD teachers will become consultants for everybody. No way. They are going to be plenty busy teaching in the classroom, especially helping those along who find school difficult. By the same token, students are going to be working, or they won't pass. Let's stop giving up on kids by maintaining an unworkable construct. The ranks of special education students are growing into an unfeasible level. Something is wrong with the present system.

Let's face it, every child is not the same. We cannot make them the same. Some have more aptitude than others in some things. Some are more skilled in some things. We educators must emphasize the value of hard work rather than emphasizing disabilities. For example, a student, we'll call him Oliver, had trouble printing early in his elementary school career. He wasn't as neat as the other kids. He began to avoid having to write anything. He hated writing. In the meantime, his classmates were practicing, doing the work, and progressing. Oliver was a very good reader. He read a lot. He even read his own books of choice. He understood symbolism and nuances of authors' intent, but when he had to take a test, or write answers to questions, he would shut down. By the time he was in 5th grade, his teachers felt he had a learning disability in written expression and reading. In middle school Oliver thought he didn't have to write because he had a learning disability. He could print in block letters, but that was about it. His teacher in middle school wasn't buying his excuses. Since he couldn't write neatly or as deftly as the other kids, he was told he had to practice more. They started with distinguishing between upper and lower case letters. Then, they worked on legibility. Oliver had great ideas and he began to put them down on paper. If he balked and didn't do the work, he didn't get any privileges. His mother was advised to have him practice at home and over the summer, which she did. His mother used to play the disability card saying he didn't have to do the amount of work that the other students did, but she changed her way of thinking because she wanted her son to improve. When her son's elementary school said he had a disability in written expression, she had bought into it at the time. With practice and desire, Oliver no longer needed special education services. This is what is meant by emphasizing hard work over a disability. If this had been done early on, there wouldn't have been the problem.

Today, there are more kids below grade level in reading than 30 years ago because of environments, choices, examples, and values. Kids watch too much TV. Their parents watch too much TV. Kids and their parents choose to sit passively instead of the mental exercises that reading provides. The brain begins to atrophy without exercise. What do parents value? Having a good time? Parents must make a commitment to stimulate their children's minds. If they don't, by the time their child reaches school age, they are not ready. They start off behind other kids who perhaps had some stimulation. They avoid reading like the plague. They get farther behind. Do they have a learning disability? Based on their performance, they must have. So, since they have a disability in reading, they don't have to read as much, so they get farther and farther behind. That kind of thinking makes *Catch-22* seem like the pinnacle of logical reasoning.

I realize that life is tough out there. Divorces, unemployment, and economic stress do not make a happy home life. If parents want children, they have got to do more for them. If Johnny can't read very well then, by God, I would take him to the library once a week for a week's supply of books for reading every night. Parents could tear themselves away from TV long enough to do that. Parents, start parenting. Students, start studying. Teachers, don't give up on kids. We can do it if we all work together.

REFERENCES

Boehm, R. G., Hoone, C., McGowan, T. M., McKinney-Browning, M. C., & Miramontes, O. B. (1997). *Our World's Story.* Orlando: Harcourt Brace.

Hardman, M. L., Drew, C. J., Egan, M. W., & Wolf, B. (1993). *Human Exceptionality.* Boston: Allyn & Bacon.

Hughes, V. (2001, July 25). Don't Know Much About History. *The Cedar Rapids Gazette.* A, p. 4.

Larson, R.E., Boswell, L., Kanold, T., & Stiff, L. (1996). *Passport to algebra and geometry.* Evanston: McDougal Littell.

Leiva, M.A., Brown, R.G., et.al. (1997) *Algebra 1: explorations and applications.* Evanston: McDougal Littell.

Mercer, C.D. (1987). *Students with learning disabilities* (3rd ed.), Columbus, OH: Merrill.

Morrison, E. S., Moore, A., Armour, N., Hammond, A. Haysom, J., Nicoll, E., & Smyth, M. (1997). *Science Plus.* Austin: Holt, Rinehart & Winston.

Mueller, A. (1999, August 23). Cedar Rapids community schools memo re IDEA 97 regulations.

Rorholm, J. (2002, March 28). Hundreds sign petition seeking audit of C.R. school district. *The Cedar Rapids Gazette.* B, p. 1.

Sleeter, C. E. (1986). Learning disabilities: the social construction of a special education category. *Exceptional Children, 53,* 46-54.

Soifer, D. (2002, June 30). Too many students are "misplaced" in special ed. *The Cedar Rapids Gazette.* A, p. 11.

Printed in the United States
107641LV00004B/2/A

9 781413 713640